BEYOND THE TEMPLE
PENTECOSTAL SPIRITUALITY AS A LIVED ECCLESIOLOGY

BEYOND THE TEMPLE

PENTECOSTAL SPIRITUALITY
AS A LIVED ECCLESIOLOGY

WILMER ESTRADA-CARRASQUILLO

CPT

CPT Press
Cleveland, Tennessee

Beyond the Temple
Pentecostal Spirituality as a Lived Ecclesiology

Published by CPT Press
900 Walker ST NE
Cleveland, TN 37311
USA
email: cptpress@pentecostaltheology.org
website: www.cptpress.com

Library of Congress Control Number: 2021942400

ISBN-13: 9781953358172

CONTENTS

PREFACE

Recently, I was talking to a longtime friend about this project. In the conversation, I said something like, 'It all started as a dissertation and now it will be in book form'. His reply was, 'That is awesome, but I believe things started way earlier, right?' After that conversation, I have played those words repeatedly; and the more I think about it, his words ring true.

Although I wrote this project while pursuing a PhD degree at Asbury Theological Seminary, the seeds of the book were planted 'way earlier'. The first seeds were planted within the Estrada Carrasquillo household, as I saw my parents model a Christian lifestyle that did not bifurcate belief and life. Consequently, those seeds were nurtured by leaders, mentors, friends, and family who constantly reminded me of God's calling in my life. Finally, throughout my graduate and post-graduate journey, I was blessed by instructors and supervisors – especially Steven Ybarrola – who helped me care for the seeds in ways that I did not know I could do. Hence, though my name may be on the cover of this book, I am mindful that whatever I say is shaped by the testimonies of a great cloud of witnesses. Nevertheless, for whatever you see lacking, I take full responsibility.

But this book is not only a testimony of my past. I pray that it has repercussions for today and for tomorrow. In the last year and a half, many church buildings closed their doors due to the pandemic. However, our inability to gather as a community of faith – vital as it is – does not presuppose that our ecclesiologies are on hold. Contrary to that, because we are temples of the Holy Spirit, our present times call for a *living ecclesiology* that is enacted in and through our bodies (1 Cor. 6.19). And in doing so, we become beacons of God's kingdom.

Finally, though I recognized the contributions of many, it is important for me mention a few. I begin by extending a word of gratitude to the administration, staff, faculty, and student body at the Pentecostal Theological Seminary and the Centre for Pentecostal Theology; your hospitality and companionship made a difference. Also, to Laura, Kalani Sofía, Mía Kamila, and Valeria Kamil; your love and support were crucial. And to the 'only God, who makes things grow'

(1 Cor. 3.7); what others planted and watered, you made what it is today.

Wilmer Estrada-Carrasquillo
Cleveland, TN

1

INTRODUCTION

A Family's Testimony

On April 19, 1999, a live bomb that was supposed to hit a US Navy restricted and targeted area for military practice, mistakenly hit an observation point and killed a civilian worker named David Sanes Rodríguez.[1] David's death unleashed a chain of events that culminated in the development of a Puerto Rican civil movement that aimed at the cessation of all naval practices on the island of Vieques, PR.[2] Almost a year after David's death, my father, who was an active participant in the civil movement, asked my siblings and me to meet him and my mother at the family room. What he said that evening has taken me on a journey in search of what it means to be a Pentecostal in the world.

To that point, our family firmly believed in the purpose and goal of the civil movement. Furthermore, we stood behind our father as he actively joined the cause and later became the spokesperson for *La Coalición Ecuménica Pro Vieques* (The Ecumenical Coalition in Favor

---

[1] Much of the land in Vieques was restricted and used by the US Navy for military purposes. Some areas were used for military practices, both by air and land. That day, according to the reports, a fighter pilot 'became disoriented at dusk and picked the wrong target' and following the confirmation of the ground control officer, dropped the '500-pound bombs' over the observation point where security guard, David Sanes Rodríguez was on duty. See, http://www.nytimes.com/1999/08/03/us/navy-attributes-fatal-bombing-to-mistakes.html (accessed June 28, 2017).

[2] This public protest was not the first Puerto Rican civil movement that stood against US military powers. During the 1960s and 1970s, Puerto Ricans protested similar practices taking place on another Puerto Rican island, Culebra.

of Vieques).[3] However, that Sunday evening, we were asked to affirm our public engagement in a way that would raise questions from our local church, our denominational leaders, and some factions of the broader society. My father informed us that he was going to cross into the US Marine restricted area in Vieques as an act of civil disobedience.[4] As soon as he finished, we all looked at *mami* (mom), and she sealed the night be affirming my dad as she said: '*yo no podré ir contigo pero estaré orando por ti para que todo salga bien*' ('I cannot go with you, but I will pray for all to go well with you'). We all understood the consequences of affirming such actions. Nevertheless, regardless of what others would say, we supported him.

My Pentecostal experience began before I stepped into a church building. I grew up in a Pentecostal household.[5] In other words, my Pentecostal experience was not mainly circumscribed to a local church; I was shaped as I sat in the living room, walked by the kitchen, or slept in my bedroom. Simply stated, all that I did or did not do was informed by a certain form of Pentecostalism. Daily, I could listen to a prayer, a song, a conversation, etc., that mentioned the Holy Spirit and the importance of its agency in our lives.[6] Much of this came from my mother's lips. In a way, her Pentecostal spirituality moved seamlessly from the church to her everyday life as if there was no dichotomy between the private and the public. Furthermore, I also heard and saw how the challenges that came from society

---

[3] This coalition, formed by a group of leaders from various religious denominations and organizations in Puerto Rico, felt called to come together and walk alongside the people of the island of Vieques as they entreated the United States of America to cease all naval practices on the island.

[4] Civil disobedience can be defined as the refusal to obey the law in certain circumstances due to its immorality. For Thoreau, it is to act like humans with conscience and not as subjects of the law. See Henry D. Thoreau, 'Civil Disobedience', 1849, http://thoreau.eserver.org/civil1.html.

[5] Though *mami* (my mother) grew up Catholic, she began to attend a Pentecostal church during her late teens in New York. *Papi* (my father) grew up in a home in which his parents had embraced Pentecostalism prior to his birth. Not only were both active members in their churches, but they were also called into ministry early in life and since then have been active ministers for the *Iglesia de Dios* Mission Board (IDDMB) of Puerto Rico (Church of God – Cleveland). The children in my family of origin – Willie, Keila, Wallie, and myself – were all born as our parents served as pastors in the IDDMB of Puerto Rico.

[6] I can still hear *mami* singing the following *corito* as she was doing her chores around the house: '*Donde está el Espíritu de Dios, hay libertad; donde está el Espíritu de Dios, hay libertad; ahí siempre hay libertad ...*' ('Where the Spirit of the Lord is, there is freedom').

pushed back against our Pentecostal beliefs.[7] This I owe to my father. Complementing what I had received from *mami* (mom), *papi's* (dad's) Pentecostal spirituality was constantly shaped by his lived realities. His context was central to his belief system. In a way, what I was receiving from my parents was: (1) that our faith is intrinsically connected to our contexts; and (2) our contexts are a soil where our faith should be rooted. Interestingly, as I grew older, I understood how what I saw and heard in the intimacy of our home was also experienced in and through our local Pentecostal congregation.[8] To borrow a term from Latin American theology, I grew up with an *integral* understanding of what it means to be Pentecostal.[9] Such a Pentecostal spirituality informed not only how I approached God in worship but also how that worship informed my lifestyle.

Theology and Anthropology

As you can see, my formation as a Pentecostal believer is nurtured by the integration of belief and practice – in other words, I learned how to *vivir entre el templo y la ciudad* ('live between the temple and the city'). Both then and now, I can still affirm such integral spirituality. In short, that is how I have come to understand the spirituality and the public: they are not mutually exclusive but, on the contrary, dialogical in nature.[10] Rather than dichotomizing these two areas, this book follows a pneumatological cultural framework, that proposes a wholistic

---

[7] AM frequency news stations were not strangers in *Papi's* car. As a result, he will normally take time during advertisement breaks, to comment about the news he heard from his Pentecostal perspective. Many times, I would hear him say, '*Como pentecostales, no podemos quedarnos callados*' ('as Pentecostals we cannot stay silent'), and that was the introduction to a long conversation about church and society.

[8] Or at least, that was what my parents tried to embody as pastors.

[9] *Integral* can be defined as holistic, wholistic, or integral. For example, to understand how *misión integral* and Pentecostalism relate to each other see, C. René Padilla, *Misión integral: Ensayos sobre el reino y la iglesia* (Grand Rapids, MI: Eerdmans, 1986); Darío López Rodríguez, *Pentecostalismo y misión integral: Teología del espíritu, teología de la vida* (Lima: Ediciones Puma, 2008).

[10] Though this dialogical nature is common in all theological approaches (Western or non-Western), I understand that Majority World theologies can provide vivid examples of such integration. For example, see Justo L. González and Ondina E. González, *Christianity in Latin America: A History* (New York: Cambridge University Press, 2007); Ogbu U. Kalu (ed.), *African Christianity: An African Story* (Trenton, NJ: Africa World Press, 2007); Samuel Hugh Moffett, *A History of Christianity in Asia: Beginnings to 1500* (Maryknoll, NY: Orbis Books, 2nd edn, 1998). A careful reading of these books underscores the *dialogical* interplay of faith and the public space.

and fluid understanding of faith and the public space and examines how they are mutually informed.

The previous statement raises the need for an integrative methodology between theological and anthropological inquiry. The former is concerned with *what* a certain community believes. The latter concentrates on *how* that which is believed *informs* the community members' practices as they interact within a specific context. In the following paragraphs, I will explain why an integrative and interdisciplinary approach is not only fitting, but even more, why it is needed.[11]

Our doing of theology is only possible thanks to God's self-revelation – as created beings, we are invited into communion with the preexisting community of the Trinity as we theologize.[12] In other words, God's self-revelation does not discourage human responses; on the contrary, it nurtures and promotes them. As a result, this act of self-revelation provides a foundation from which humanity constructs its theological understanding of God. Here lies the crux of the divine-human interaction of theology: that God's initiating activity does not presuppose the negation of human participation; rather, it opens a space for it. Humanity is invited to participate in the community of God; and such participation is transmitted through humanly constructed thought, or as Rowan Williams states, 'in the context of our ordinary ways of making sense of things'.[13]

In this sense theology is contextual. It considers and addresses the needs and matters that arise in a certain place and context. In the words of Frank Macchia, 'being contextual means engaging

---

[11] In his award-winning work, Stanley Skreslet emphasizes that studies on theology and mission cannot be taken seriously if they are not done with an interdisciplinary focus. For an in-depth discussion, see Stanley H. Skreslet, *Comprehending Mission: The Questions, Methods, Themes, Problems, and Prospects of Missiology* (American Society of Missiology Series 49; Maryknoll, NY: Orbis Books, 2012), p. 14.

[12] Speaking about God's self-revelation and adaptation to human speech, van Engen states, 'Since God spoke to Adam and Eve in the Garden we can appreciate God's adaptation to human cultures in communicating God's intended meaning, the forms God chose to communicate with humans, and the spiritual power struggles between God's desires for humanity and human sinfulness'. See Charles Edward van Engen, 'Preface', in Charles Edward van Engen, Darrell L. Whiteman, and John Dudley Woodberry (eds.), *Paradigm Shifts in Christian Witness: Insights from Anthropology, Communication, and Spiritual Power: Essays in Honor of Charles H. Kraft* (Maryknoll, NY: Orbis Books, 2008), p. xv.

[13] For an interesting study of the role of language in our Christian experience, see Rowan Williams, *The Edge of Words: God and the Habits of Language* (London: Bloomsbury, 2014), p. 3.

theologically one's milieu: where God's story of the world meets our big and little stories at a particular time and place'.[14] Following Macchia's statement, it can be affirmed that the task of theologizing is an integrative event between God, context, and human experiences. Furthermore, and similarly to Macchia's point, Timothy Tennent argues that 'the gospel is culturally and geographically translatable – that is, it has found new homes in a vast number of cultures and places'.[15] In this sense, regardless of our cultural and confessional backgrounds, theology is a divinely initiated experience that invites humanity to worship God's self-revelation in history through speech and actions from our contextual realities.

Theology, prior to being a set of articulated propositions, is a 'lived experience'.[16] Hence, theology occurs 'as the church lives out its given script in new situations'.[17] Now, this does not mean that experience is preferred or that the articulation of theology is rejected. As a matter of fact, both are important for the theological task and the testimony of the Christian tradition, especially when context is taken seriously, as in this study.[18] Perhaps it is safe to say that ecclesial studies benefits from this integrative nature. On the one hand, literature (e.g. confessional, denominational, or that coming from trained theologians) preserves the teachings and practices that identify a certain community of faith or Christianity in general. On the other hand, beliefs are not only read but are also lived and enacted. This tension

---

[14] Frank Macchia, 'Systematic Theology', in William A. Dyrness *et al.*, (eds.), *Global Dictionary of Theology: A Resource for the Worldwide Church* (Downers Grove, IL: IVP Academic, 2008), p. 866.

[15] Expanding on this point, Tennent adds, 'Christian faith is not only *culturally* translatable, it is also *theologically* translatable. I am defining theological translatability as *the ability of the kerygmatic essentials of the Christian faith to be discovered and restated within an infinite number of new global contexts*'. See Timothy C. Tennent, *Theology in the Context of World Christianity: How the Global Church Is Influencing the Way We Think about and Discuss Theology* (Grand Rapids, MI: Zondervan, 2007), p. 16.

[16] Simon Chan, *Grassroots Asian Theology: Thinking the Faith from the Ground Up* (Downers Grove, IL: InterVarsity Press, 2014), p. 15.

[17] Simon Chan, *Grassroots Asian Theology*, p. 15.

[18] Following this line of thought, Gregg A. Okesson states, 'Theology should not operate solely with *professional* theologians but occurs as people think about God, themselves, and their relationship with the world'. See Gregg A. Okesson, *Re-Imaging Modernity: A Contextualized Theological Study of Power and Humanity within Akamba Christianity in Kenya* (American Society of Missiology Monograph Series 16; Eugene, OR: Pickwick Publications, 2012), p. 38.

is at the crux of the Pentecostal community, as Pentecostals claim to be people of the Book and people of the Spirit. The problem arises when we are not able to maintain a healthy tension between these two marks and one becomes the norm.[19] Thus, to avoid the pitfall of favoring one over the other and to keep in line with the integrative methodology, this study seeks to nuance theological discourses (literary research) with concrete experiences (empirical research).[20]

One scholar who has modeled this integrative approach within Pentecostal studies and intercultural studies is Mark Cartledge. Though the bulk of his work has been studying Pentecostal and charismatic churches in the United Kingdom and now in the United States, his methodological approach is useful beyond these contexts.[21] For Cartledge, there are various reasons for the integration of empirical research in ecclesial studies. He begins by saying, 'both [theological and empirical research] approaches stress the nature of theology in terms of narrative'.[22] Second, 'both approaches wish to give priority to local voices'.[23] Third, 'both approaches are interested in the church'.[24] Fourth, 'both are interested in spirituality'.[25]

---

[19] Sadly, in general, theology as a theological articulation is favored over theology as a lived experience.

[20] See Mark J. Cartledge, 'Renewal Ecclesiology in Empirical Perspective', *Pneuma* 36 (2014), p. 24.

[21] For a description of how his work has developed the last eighteen years, see his most recent book: Mark J. Cartledge, *Narratives and Numbers: Empirical Studies of Pentecostal and Charismatic Christianity* (Global Pentecostal and Charismatic Studies 24; Boston: Brill, 2017).

[22] Mark J. Cartledge, 'Pentecostal Theological Method and Intercultural Theology', *Transformation* 25.2/3 (April 2008), p. 98.

[23] However, Cartledge also recognizes that they express them in different ways. 'The Pentecostal method offers this through community testimony and group prayer meetings, while the Intercultural method uses indigenous categories to critique and challenge Western categories'. Cartledge, 'Pentecostal Theological Method and Intercultural Theology', 99.

[24] Similar to the local voice element, though they give importance to the local church, their understanding of ecclesiology differs. On the one hand, Pentecostals have a bounded understanding of the community. On the other hand, intercultural studies has a more broad or open definition of community. See, Cartledge, 'Pentecostal Theological Method and Intercultural Theology', p. 99.

[25] Interestingly, Pentecostals place spirituality 'at the heart of the process of doing theology'. See, Cartledge, 'Pentecostal Theological Method and Intercultural Theology', p. 99.

A Trialectical Conversation: Pentecostal, Contextual, and Public Theologies

The integrative methodology between theology and anthropology is framed with a trialectical conversation between Pentecostal, contextual, and public theologies. These loci have been present, with some variations, throughout Christian history. However, they gained scholarly popularity during the twentieth century. While each one has a unique lens from which it operates, having the twentieth century as their common seedbed ties them together in ways never before experienced. The following paragraphs attests to their interconnectivity and utility for this study.

At the dawn of the twentieth century, Christianity enjoyed the status of being the largest religious movement in the world, particularly established in and dominated by the West. Nevertheless, as the century unfolded, Christianity's center of gravity moved from the West toward the Majority World.[26] Interestingly, although it was described as 'the most remarkable century in the history of the expansion of Christianity', scholars also recognized that though 'Christianity began the twentieth century as a Western religion … it ended the century as a non-Western religion, on track to become progressively more so'.[27] Consensus across the academy has recognized that various elements have contributed to this shift, including the following: (1) political instability – many of the world's more stable nations were under siege due to the various wars that erupted; (2) human tragedy – the product of fatal events such as the world wars, the Holocaust, and nuclear bombings; (3) social activism – gender, race, and peace manifestations were transformative events; (4) the fall of communism – one of the central events of the late twentieth century; (5) nationalistic sentiments – many nations under the oppression of colonial powers began to seek independence; and (6) the relationship of church and state – there was no unified model. As a result, the instability created by

---

[26] See, for example, Philip Jenkins, *The Next Christendom: The Coming of Global Christianity* (Oxford: Oxford UP, 3rd edn, 2011). In this book, Jenkins examines the metamorphosis of Christianity from the Western bastion to the Majority World phenomena.

[27] Andrew F. Walls, *The Cross-Cultural Process in Christian History: Studies in the Transmission and Appropriation of Faith* (Maryknoll, NY: Orbis Books, 2002), p. 64.

these sociopolitical events unveiled a cruel reality: 'The moral pretensions of the West were shown to be a sham'.[28]

Against this backdrop, we encounter the inevitable flourishing of Pentecostal, contextual, and public theologies. Their rise during such an unstable era stands as a testimony of the *restoration, reimagination,* and *resistance* of Christian theology and praxis: all three loci embody such descriptors. Their commonalities are not due to coincidence, but such trialectical symbiosis is nurtured by the place and space from which they flourish. Unfortunately, the specialization and compartmentalization that permeates in academia predisposes us to see these loci as mutually exclusive rather than integrated.

Nevertheless, this study proposes the contrary. As happens among siblings, each has traits that are unique while other traits affirm their relatedness. In the conjunction of both their uniqueness and relatedness we find that which holds them together. Something similar happens with these theological perspectives. Despite their indigeneity, there are contributing elements that interconnect each with the others and make possible the trialectical relationship among the three.

Early Pentecostal literature establishes that factions of the Pentecostal movement seamlessly integrate their beliefs with their practices. Such integral character, accompanied by the infilling of the Holy Spirit, has fueled Pentecostals' contextual and public presence. Accordingly, Pentecostals have made their impact among the most oppressed and marginalized sectors of society. By doing so, Pentecostalism heightens the importance of the context of those whom they serve and becomes a beacon of hope and social transformation within the market square.[29]

Furthermore, contextual theology provides a framework that underscores the importance of the concrete realities of believers as they engage the gospel. Without questioning the transculturality of the gospel, contextual theology empowers believers to engage God from the ground up. Such an approach not only opened a space for the voices of the Majority World and minorities in the West, it also served as a catalyst for social unrest and public engagement. Similarly,

---

[28] Stephen Neill, *A History of Christian Missions* (ed. Owen Chadwick; New York: Penguin Books, 1990), p. 416.

[29] See, for example, Wilfredo Estrada Adorno, *El fuego está encendido: Infancia del pentecostalismo puertorriqueño y su impacto en la sociedad* (Cleveland, TN: CEL Publicaciones, 2016).

Pentecostals affirm that the Holy Spirit will fall upon believers despite their ethnicity, gender, class, or background. In other words, there is a recognition of the person and its contexts. Regardless of their social condition, the Holy Spirit empowers and gives them a voice for the edification of the church and for the engagement with public issues.

Finally, public theology could be defined as the embodiment of faith in a common space for the sake of the betterment of the city. This occurs as public theology unfolds in context. In other words, to be effective, those seeking to theologize in the common space need to understand the signs of the times and act accordingly. Following this line of thought, it can be affirmed that Pentecostalism has had a public character. Many Pentecostals, past and present, have understood the work of the Holy Spirit as liberating: that is, incarnated in the perils, trials, and difficulties of the people and standing against the powers of this world and advocating for the restoration and welfare of those in need.

How does this trialectical interplay of Pentecostal, contextual, and public theologies inform the proposed thesis? Pentecostal ecclesiology is directly and indirectly informed by all three loci. On the one hand, we recognize *el culto* (Pentecostal service) as one locus. On the other hand, we cannot overlook the lived spaces (the context and public space) where Pentecostal believers live *in* and embody their faith. They go hand-in-hand.

The relationship between *el culto* (worship service) and the community is key. When the church gathers, she ministers *to* and *with* the community of the believers. Furthermore, she ministers *from* and *for* their communities. Hence, to understand her prophetic call, to be an *ekklesia* – not only as an identity marker but also through embodiment – it is important to have an idea of the societal contexts where she is planted. In other words, theology is the product of the interaction between the church community and the community where she is rooted.[30] Such appropriation affirms the Pentecostal and Latin American character of the church. This study is concerned with both. Regarding the character of Pentecostal theology and spirituality, John

---

[30] For an example of the relationship of the theologian and the church, see Robert J Schreiter, *Constructing Local Theologies* (Maryknoll, NY: Orbis Books, 1985).

Christopher Thomas states the following in his Society for Pentecostal Studies (SPS) presidential address:

> For Pentecostal theology to be informed and shaped by the Pentecostal community is more than an acknowledgment that Pentecostal theologians should be church attendees or conversant with the theology of the tradition. Rather, it is a confession of the extremely tight interplay that must exist between the ethos of the tradition and the work of those called to discover, construct, and articulate its theology.[31]

In like manner, speaking from a Latin American perspective, Daniel Chiquete states the following regarding the Latin American aspect: 'Liturgical experiences emerge from spatial, social and ecclesial contexts. This is how they can reflect the cultural values of their particular society, along with motifs and attitudes, which are related to the symbolic universe of the religious community.'[32] Hence, it is extremely important to pay attention to how these loci become formative within the Pentecostal community and how they are embodied in the public sphere.

Significance of the Study

This study attempts to construct a Pentecostal lived ecclesiology by exploring how lived faith informs the way people interact in their lived spaces. To some extent, Pentecostals have been portrayed as anticultural and unworried about this-worldly events. Yet this study is significant for how it reveals that there are Pentecostal voices and churches that are seriously thinking about the ways that their spirituality impacts the public sphere.

Second, as a lived religion, Pentecostalism needs to 'revision' itself constantly. Much of the *revisioning* project among classical Pentecostals has been slow in treating the topic of theology and culture.[33]

---

[31] John Christopher Thomas, 'Pentecostal Theology in the Twenty-First Century', *Pneuma* 20.1 (1998), p. 7.

[32] Daniel Chiquete, *Silencio elocuente: una interpretación de la arquitectura pentecostal* (San José, Costa Rica: Univ. Bíblica Latinoamericana, 2006), p. 51. My translation.

[33] In what is known as a seminal book on Pentecostal theology, Steven J. Land states, 'What is needed is a revision of the old models, a reappraisal of dispensational association, an integration of soteriological "experiences", a concerted effort toward unity and inclusiveness, and an expanded definition of mission which will move Pentecostalism away from some of the more individualistic understandings

Thus, this study fills a void within Pentecostal and broader Christian literature.

Furthermore, this study seeks to make a much-needed contribution within the area of public missiology.[34] To become more attuned to the public space not only makes the church more relevant, but, more importantly, it also makes the church more attuned to its context and will open new avenues for missiological engagement. The church, as ambassadors of Christ in this world, is responsible for knowing the times, the narratives of today's culture, and for being capable of translating the gospel in fresh ways.

Finally, for Allan Anderson, there is a deep integration between Pentecostalism and mission. He states, 'Just as Spirit baptism is Pentecostalism's central, most distinctive doctrine, so mission is Pentecostalism's central, most important activity'.[35] I truly believe that Latino/a Pentecostals are spearheading such integration by constantly asking themselves how their theology shapes and informs their public engagement, and vice versa. Thus, drawing from Latino/a Pentecostal literature and Puerto Rican Pentecostal ecclesial practice, this study seeks to propose a Pentecostal lived ecclesiology.

Outline of Chapters

The fundamental question of this study is, how do Pentecostals approach the interplay of church and society and what theological and

---

of the past'. Some of examples of this Pentecostal revisioning are mentioned below. Rather than exhaustive, this serves as a representative list: Steven Jack Land, *Pentecostal Spirituality: A Passion for the Kingdom* (1993; repr., Cleveland, TN: CPT Press, 2010), 195–96; Kimberly Ervin Alexander, *Pentecostal Healing: Models in Theology and Practice* (JPTSup 29; Blandford Forum, UK: Deo Publishing, 2006); Archer, *A Pentecostal Hermeneutic*; Cheryl Bridges Johns, *Pentecostal Formation: A Pedagogy among the Oppressed* (JPTSup 2; Sheffield: Sheffield Academic Press, 1993); John Christopher Thomas, *Toward a Pentecostal Ecclesiology: The Church and the Fivefold Gospel* (Cleveland, TN: CPT Press, 2010); Chris E.W. Green, *Toward a Pentecostal Theology of the Lord's Supper: Foretasting the Kingdom* (Cleveland, TN: CPT Press, 2012); Tony Richie, *Toward a Pentecostal Theology of Religions: Encountering Cornelius Today* (Cleveland, TN: CPT Press, 2013).

[34] Though it is safe to say that mission has always been intrinsically connected to the public realm, the work of Lesslie Newbigin has been instrumental in planting the foundation for the development of public missiology. In the following chapter, this area of study will be further developed. See for example, Lesslie Newbigin, *The Gospel in a Pluralist Society* (Grand Rapids, MI: Eerdmans, 1989); George R. Hunsberger, *Bearing the Witness of the Spirit: Lesslie Newbigin's Theology of Cultural Plurality* (The Gospel and Our Culture Series; Grand Rapids, MI: Eerdmans, 1998).

[35] Allan Anderson, *Spreading Fires: The Missionary Nature of Early Pentecostalism* (Maryknoll, NY: Orbis Books, 2007), p. 65.

missiological contributions do we bring to this topic? Whether I am able to fulfil such a task lies in the chapters that follow. Hence, as a matter of an introduction I will briefly sketch each chapter.

Chapter 2 lays out the biblical, theological, and contextual foundations of the study. The chapter begins by offering a reading of Ezekiel's vision of the temple found in ch. 47. I will argue that this vision reiterates the close relationship that exists between lived faith and lived spaces.

Chapter 3 examines the literary contributions of three Latino/a Pentecostal theologians: Agustina Luvis, Eldin Villafañe, and Darío López. The theologians will be engaged in the following way: a brief biographical description; a description of their ecclesial theologies; and then an analysis of how their ecclesial theologies contribute to the development of a lived ecclesiology. As it will be noted, all three theologians underscore the integral character of the Pentecostal movement and understand that the local church plays a major role in this task of affirming Pentecostalism's public character.

Chapter 4 presents a case study which seeks to describe how the Latino/a Pentecostal church integrates her lived faith with her lived spaces. This empirical study mixes participant observation with focus group interviews as its primary ethnographic tools. I present not only their collective songs, prayers, testimonies, sermons, and readings but also their particular voices regarding how their local church (*Iglesia de Dios Mission Board 'Ríos de Agua Viva'*) and their Pentecostal experience has (in)formed their public character.

In Chapter 5, by way of integration, I attempt to construct a Pentecostal lived ecclesiology that is informed by Pentecostal theory and praxis. First, in dialogue with Pentecostal scholarship, I propose a Pentecostal method for a lived ecclesiology. This method is developed by synthesizing the contributions of a representative group of Pentecostal theologians. Then, taking into consideration this method along with the findings of the previous chapters, I describe four major themes (conversion *from* and *to*; an integral spirituality; prayer and intercession as missiological in nature; and the prophethood of all) that arise from the integration of the contributions from Luvis, Villafañe, López, and the case study.

Finally, the book concludes by offering some contributions and findings that might be of interest for further study.

2

DO YOU SEE?!

Water Running from the Temple

As stated in the previous chapter, the Pentecostal experience in which I was nurtured overlapped spirituality and daily life experiences, the city and the church. According to Steven J. Land, this integration is part of our Pentecostal DNA. Land states, 'The Pentecostal concern is that as of Paul in 1 Corinthians 12 *—to emphasize the lived reality of the faith, the life and service of the people of God who are organically constituted as the body of Christ by the indwelling of the Holy Spirit*.[1] If my reading of Land is correct, it seems that for him, those who are indwelled by the Holy Spirit not only become Christ's embodiment here on Earth, but also there is a Spirited-passion that brings forth an *integration of faith and life*. As I reflected on this, I began to meditate on biblical images that could help me describe the *living* spirituality informing my Pentecostal experience. Though various biblical narratives came to mind, the one that kept recurring and moving to the foreground was that of Ezek. 47.1-12.

The remainder of this chapter offers a reading of Ezekiel's vision of the waters running from the temple. Subsequently, I will discuss how this narrative serves as a foundation for the study in hand. However, I understand that it will be helpful to begin by briefly describing a Pentecostal way of reading scripture. As you may imagine, this approach is also informed by my Latino experience.

---

[1] Land, *Pentecostal Spirituality*, p. 21. Emphasis added.

A Pentecostal Latino Reading

Our reading of the Word of God does not happen in a vacuum. It is informed by the conscious and unconscious preconceptions that are part of our *social imagination*.[2] Among those that inform my social imagination, I will focus on two of them, Pentecostal, and Latino. Though our ethnic identities usually precede our faith confessions, I intentionally placed Pentecostal first, because as I reflected on my Christian experience, I recognized that I *consciously* read scripture with my Pentecostal lenses, before I did as a Latino. Of course, I am Puerto Rican, and I primarily read the *Bibla en español*, yet it was not a conscious reading. Actually, I did not understand the importance and the profitableness of reading scripture as a Puerto Rican or Latino until I experienced a life away from home.[3]

A Pentecostal Hermeneutic?

For Pentecostals the Bible is the Word of God. Through it the *reader* is able to *hear* God's voice. This approach to scripture understands the Word of God as a living Word. As a result, Pentecostals read the Bible not as a static event but on the contrary, as an event that is both 'dynamic and active'.[4] Thus, instead of approaching the word in search of propositional truths, a Pentecostal reading of scripture seeks to foster a charged space of encounter between God and the readers/hearers.

Furthermore, it can be added that a Pentecostal reading of the scripture is guided by a narrative approach (this does not mean that other hermeneutical approaches are rejected). Because the scripture is a dynamic text, there is a sense of ontological and teleological connectivity from Genesis to Revelation and vice versa. This is why, in part, as John Christopher Thomas states, that 'Pentecostals avoid a canon within the canon approach by taking seriously the theological

---

[2] Charles Taylor, *Modern Social Imaginaries* (Durham: Duke University Press Books, 2003).

[3] For a detailed narrative about my experience in the North American diaspora see, Néstor Medina and Sammy Alfaro (eds.), *Pentecostals and Charismatics in Latin America and Latino Communities* (Christianity and Renewal-Interdisciplinary Studies; New York: Palgrave Macmillan, 2015); Wilmer Estrada-Carrasquillo, *Hacia una eclesiología hispana-latina: Una respuesta al reto de la mcdonalización* (Cleveland, TN: CEL Publicaciones, 2019).

[4] John Christopher Thomas, 'Pentecostal Interpretation' in Steven L. McKenzie (ed.), *The Oxford Encyclopedia of Biblical Interpretation* (Oxford; New York: Oxford University Press, 2013), p. 89.

dimension of *all* scripture'.[5] Now, this narrative is not a distant narrative. On the contrary, led by the agency of the Holy Spirit, we immerse ourselves in the story in ways that God's story is weaved into ours. In other words, the world of scripture and our worlds overlap. Hence, through the Holy Spirit, we are capable of placing ourselves in the biblical stories and participate as the individual/community is living it out.[6] Such an event places Pentecostals in a unique place, a place where we 'experience' God[7] and a place where we 'encounter Christ'.[8]

In many cases, Pentecostals may express these experiences and encounters with the living Word of God through testimonies. In these written and spoken oracles we can attest the truest example of how the scripture turns out to be, as Cheryl Bridges Johns says, 'an avenue for us to enter into the mysterious, wonder-filled life of God'.[9] These testimonies are important for Pentecostal hermeneutics. They serve as a window into the ways God has impacted the life of an individual/community and to the way scripture has been interpreted in light of their lived experiences. Hence, a Pentecostal hermeneutic cannot be done in isolation from the ways the community has understood scripture, but on the contrary, it is important 'to hear and be (in)formed by the voices' of our Pentecostal brothers and sisters.[10]

This brief description of a Pentecostal interpretation of scriptures, underscores what Amos Yong calls 'trialectical interrelationality'.[11] That is, an integrative relationship between the Word, the Holy Spirit, and the community.[12]

---

[5] Thomas, 'Pentecostal Interpretation', p. 89.

[6] Thomas, 'Pentecostal Interpretation', p. 90.

[7] Melissa L. Archer, *'I Was in the Spirit on the Lord's Day': A Pentecostal Engagement with Worship in the Apocalypse* (Cleveland, TN: CPT Press, 2015).

[8] Chris E.W. Green, *Sanctifying Interpretation: Vocation, Holiness, and Scripture* (Cleveland, TN: CPT Press, 2015), p. 115.

[9] Cheryl Bridges Johns, 'Grieving, Brooding, and Transforming', *Journal of Pentecostal Theology* 23.2 (October 2014), p. 148.

[10] David R. Johnson, *Pneumatic Discernment in the Apocalypse: An Intertextual and Pentecostal Exploration* (Cleveland, TN: CPT Press, 2018), pp. 26–27.

[11] Amos Yong, *Spirit, Word, Community: Theological Hermeneutics in Trinitarian Perspective* (Eugene, OR: Wipf & Stock, 2006), p. 219.

[12] Explaining the relation to each other, Yong states, 'Herein lies the relational, perichoretic and robustly trinitarian nature of the hermeneutical trialectic of interpretative acts (Spirit), interpretative objects (Word), and interpretative contexts (Community)'. See, Yong, *Spirit, Word, Community*, p. 220.

A Latino Hermeneutic?

In *Making Room*, Christine Pohl shares that there are things that we will never be able to understand in full until we become the *Other*. It seems that putting ourselves in a place of vulnerability opens areas of our lives that are hidden to us. Accordingly, my Latino reading did not become unhidden until I experienced what it was to be the *other* in a strange land. This *concientización*[13] occurred as I began to read and hear the stories of my Latino sisters and brothers that preceded me in this journey in the US. This new reality opened a new way of reading the living Word of God (*la palabra de Dios*). In words of Orlando Costas, I experienced a 'cultural conversion'.[14] For Costas, this became a central hermeneutical key.

Similarly, Justo González was another voice that helped me understand the importance of reading the Bible in Spanish. However, this call is more than just using a Bible that is translated in Spanish, in the words of González,

> What I mean is more than that: If it is true that we bring a particular experience to history and to theology, then we must also bring a *particular perspective* to the interpretation of Scripture. And, once again, it may be that this perspective will prove useful not only to us but also to the church at large.[15]

This perspective calls for a particular reading and not a mere translation of language. A Latino reading of Scripture calls for new grammars. These grammars, according to González are, 'power and powerlessness', a communal interpretation of the Bible, reading it with the mindset of the *least of these*, and that the study of 'Scripture it is

---

[13] For an in-depth study of the usage of the term conscientization from Latino and Pentecostal perspectives see the following works. Paulo Freire, *Pedagogy of the Oppressed* (New York: Continuum, 30th Anniv. edn, 2000); Johns, *Pentecostal Formation*; Miriam E. Figueroa Aponte, *Hacia una teología pentecostalista: Mujeres impulsadas por el Espíritu Santo* (CEL Publicaciones, 2016).

[14] For Costas, conversion has various levels. This first can be described as his 'religious conversion'. The second level refers to his 'cultural conversion'. *Through his new life in Christ he found himself as Puerto Rican and Latin American. This second level was central in his theological methodology.* Finally, the third level refers to his 'sociopolitical conversion'. He understood the centrality that the poor and the marginalized had in God's kingdom. These three levels of conversion are not isolated events, but overlapping and continuous. Orlando E. Costas, *The Integrity of Mission: The Inner Life and Outreach the Church* (San Francisco: Harper & Row, 1979), p. 9.

[15] Justo L. González, *Mañana: Christian Theology from a Hispanic Perspective* (Nashville: Abingdon Press, 1990), p. 75. Emphasis added.

not so much to interpret it as to allow it to interpret us and our situation'.[16]

Furthermore, Latino readings of Scripture are hospitable to the role that the Holy Spirit plays in such a task. In a chapter that studies how Latina women read scripture, Elizabeth Conde-Frazier says, 'the Holy Spirit enlightens the mind of the receiver of the word so that the meaning for one's life may be clear. In this way, the word not only informs and instructs but also addressed as a person.'[17] Such a reading helped Conde-Frazier, as I mentioned in the previous section, make meaning of her life as a Latina in the US. She explains, 'the Bible is read *from lived reality*, with the purpose of interpreting and finding both meaning and God in the midst of it'.[18] Another example of such a Latino hermeneutical approach is the work of biblical scholar, Rodolfo 'Rudy' Galvan Estrada. In his study of the Gospel of John, he approaches the biblical text informed by his experience as both a Pentecostal and a Latino worshiper. In it, he is able to conclude, among other things, that the Spirit serves as an advocate for/of those who are dehumanized due to their categorization as a minority.[19]

In sum, similar to Pentecostals, Latinos approach the Bible with the expectancy to read/hear God's voice. Two things are expected, on the one hand, 'a profound spiritual life' and on the other hand, an 'effective change in the life of the human being'.[20] This transformation of the individual/community is generated, as Miguel Álvarez shares, 'by the integration of the Word, the Holy Spirit and the community of faith'.[21] Interestingly, though Pentecostal and Latino hermeneutics have unique starting points in their interpretative process,

---

[16] González, *Mañana*, pp. 85–86.

[17] It is important to mention at this juncture, that Conde-Frazier is speaking here as an Evangelical. Hence, the way she describes the agency of the Holy Spirit in the interpretative process – illumination – does not describes in its entirety the greater role that Pentecostals ascribe to the Spirit. Elizabeth Conde-Frazier, 'Evangélicas Reading Scriptures: Readings from within and beyond the Tradition', in Loida I. Martell-Otero *et al.*, *Latina Evangélicas: A Theological Survey from the Margins* (Eugene, OR: Cascade Books, 2013), p. 76.

[18] Conde-Frazier, 'Evangélicas Reading Scriptures', p. 78.

[19] Rodolfo Galvan Estrada, *A Pneumatology of Race in the Gospel of John: An Ethnocritical Study* (Eugene, OR: Pickwick, 2019).

[20] Miguel Álvarez, 'Contextualización de la hermenéutica latina', *Hechos* 1.1 (2019), p. 7 (my translation).

[21] Álvarez, 'Contextualización de la hermenéutica Latina', p. 7.

what they have in common is their communal orientation, a dynamic view of the Word and the sensibility to the work of Holy Spirit.

Pentecostal Readings of Ezekiel

Compared to other books in the Old Testament, Pentecostal[22] publications on the book of Ezekiel are not as popular. Rebecca Basdeo Hill states, in her recentl work on Ezekiel, that this book 'has been virtually ignored by Pentecostals, a fact that is paradoxical considering Pentecostalism's interest in the Holy Spirit and Ezekiel's frequent mention of the Holy Spirit'.[23]

As a result, though the information available for the purpose of this study is scarce, the sample at hand serves a case study that provides a window into the particular ways Pentecostals interpreted the prophetic oracles of Ezekiel, especially that of 47.1-12.

Pentecostals and Ezekiel 47.1-12

Let me begin by making reference to how early Pentecostals treated Ezekiel's vision of the waters running from the temple. By early Pentecostals I mean, its first ten years – from 1906 to 1916.[24] I will do so by reading the sermons, testimonies, and stories that were printed in their early periodicals and other documents.

The earliest mention of Ezekiel is found in the 1909 publication of *The Bridegroom's Messenger*.[25] The author of the article, 'River of Water of Life', immediately connects this 'river of water' to the Holy Spirit. The writer, Elizabeth Sexton, states, 'but where water is used figuratively … it symbolizes more generally the Spirit's office work in human hearts'. This *connection* between the 'river of water' and the Holy Spirit, grants this river, according to Sexton, some attributes that we find in the Holy Spirit. This river 'satisfies the thirst', 'fertilizes the ground', 'becomes a source of power', 'cleanses from sin

---

[22] A. Rebecca Basdeo Hill, *Visions of God in Ezekiel: Pentecostal Explorations of the Glory and Holiness of Yahweh* (Cleveland, TN: CPT Press, 2018), pp. 13–14.

[23] Basdeo Hill, *Visions of God in Ezekiel*, p. 13.

[24] By earliest I mean what Walter Hollenweger described and Pentecostal scholars affirmed afterward as the *heart* of the movement. See for example, Walter J. Hollenweger, *Pentecostalism: Origins and Developments Worldwide* (Peabody, MA: Hendrickson Publishers, 2005).

[25] E.A.S[exton], 'Editorial: River of Water of Life', *The Bridegroom's Messenger* 3.48 (Oct 15, 1909), p. 1. This periodical was published by G.B. Cashwell in Atlanta, GA, beginning in 1907. Elizabeth A. Sexton was editor of the paper.

and pollution of sin', and it is 'necessary to the natural universe and natural man'.[26]

Following these words, Sexton explains what she understands is happening in the text as the angel is taking Ezekiel from shallow waters into the depths of the river. First, the waters to the ankles of the prophet 'suggests the walking in the "newness of life"'.[27] In other words, it means that we are being born of the Spirit. Second, the waters to the knees is the 'same Spirit that comes to quicken in the new birth, takes us deeper in God ... to be sanctified and set apart for his service'.[28] Third, the waters to the loins 'suggests strength and power ... the Holy Spirit's mighty work upon the sanctified life in Pentecostal baptism'.[29] Finally, the river is so wide and deep that it can only be passed by swimming. Here, 'the saints now stand on the brink of a grand ocean of love, too broad to pass over, too deep to fathom'.[30]

This vision of the water running from the temple stands as a *river salutis*[31] that takes a person from new birth to the fullness of life – by way of sanctification and Spirit Baptism. Though the scope and focus of this study stands elsewhere, it is important to recognize, that Sexton's understanding of the salvation follows the Wesleyan Pentecostal approach of soteriology.[32]

---

[26] S[exton], 'Editorial: River of Water of Life', p. 1.
[27] S[exton], 'Editorial: River of Water of Life', p. 1.
[28] S[exton], 'Editorial: River of Water of Life', p. 1.
[29] S[exton], 'Editorial: River of Water of Life', p. 1.
[30] S[exton], 'Editorial: River of Water of Life', p. 1.
[31] The term *river salutis* stands as a reference to the term *via salutis*. Some Pentecostal scholars adopted the use of *via salutis* instead of *ordo salutis*, to describe the 'dynamic pneumatic soteriology' of Pentecostalism and to 'show that the (Pentecostal) believer is living in the Spirit from the first moment of faith in Christ'. This stands in contrast to the *ordo salutios* coming from the reformed tradition. See Donald K. McKim, *Westminster Dictionary of Theological Terms* (Louisville, KY: Westminster John Knox Press, 1996), p. 195; R.H Gause, *Living in the Spirit: The Way of Salvation* (Cleveland, TN: CPT Press, 2009), p. 1; Kenneth J. Archer, 'Nourishment for Our Journey: The Pentecostal *Via Salutis* and Sacramental Ordiances', *Journal of Pentecostal Theology* 13.1 (October 1, 2004), p. 82.
[32] This approach is central to my Pentecostal spirituality. For a study regarding a Pentecostal understanding of the *via salutis* see, Gause, *Living in the Spirit*, pp. 1–2. In the introduction of the book Gause explains, that the receiving of the 'Holy Spirit is a distinctive experience. It is not to be confused with the experiences of initial salvation [what Sexton calls new birth]. Neither is to be confused with subsequent crisis experience of sanctification ... All of the prior experiences in redemption anticipated and culminated in baptism with the Holy Spirit.'

We find the second mention of Ezekiel 47 in *The Latter Rain Evangel* publication of June 1912.[33] The reference appears in a sermon that was preached by Miss E. Sisson during a convention in May 19, 1912. The title of the sermon was 'Blessings from Under the Threshold: The Vision of the Holy Waters'. According to Henrietta E. Muzzy, who shares her impressions of the convention in the same publication, shares that this sermon was part of a 'missionary service'.[34] In this particular occasion, Ezekiel's vision serves as a missionary call for those in attendance. Similar to the first mention, Miss E. Sisson connects the waters flowing from the temple to the Holy Spirit. Yet, in this case, those who are immersed in the waters of the Holy Spirit are submerged in a holiness of life that bears witness every place we go. Sisson exclaims,

> Oh, what holy life in the kitchen! What holy life in the office, on the street! What holy life in the bedchamber! What holy life at the dining table! What holy life when waters are to the loins! That is provided for us. Everything under, all the movement of our being under the Holy Ghost.[35]

The third occurrence of Ezekiel's vision of the water running from the temple appears in the Church of God General Assembly Minutes (Cleveland) titled 'Echoes from the Ninth Annual Assembly of the Church of God', which were published in 1913.[36] The reference to Ezekiel 47 appears during the General Overseer's Annual Address. The tone of A.J. Tomlinson's address seeks to challenge those at the assembly to understand the times when the young church was living and to recognize the need of establishing certain governing processes. Tomlinson states,

> This is not a convention for mere pleasure or pastime, neither is it expected to be like a revival or camp-meeting, but it is for the purpose of considering matters of government, and to obtain Bible knowledge which, when in perfect operation leads to more extensive revivals and greater camp-meetings.[37]

---

[33] Miss E. Sisson, 'Blessings from Under the Threshold: The Vision of the Holy Waters', *The Latter Rain Evangel* 4.9 (June 1912), p. 12.

[34] Sisson, 'Blessings from Under the Threshold', p. 12.

[35] Sisson, 'Blessings from Under the Threshold', p. 12.

[36] *Church of God General Assembly Minutes*, 1913.

[37] *Church of God General Assembly Minutes*, p. 5.

Right after this pronunciation, Tomlinson offers some examples to ratify his point. Amongst those that he mentions is that of 'evangelistic and mission work' and 'the pastoral problem'.[38] It seems that these were areas of much struggle and needed to be strengthened. Hence, Tomlinson urges his hearers to give 'your very best attention' and that it was 'better to go hungry that to leave this stone covered over with moss and dust any longer'.[39]

After highlighting the importance of these two areas, he then enters into financial matters. It is here that Ezekiel is mentioned. Tomlinson states, 'Upon this [financial matters] depends much of the success of both the evangelistic and pastoral work'.[40] In other words, the financial contributions of the members of the Church of God would be key in strengthening the church's evangelistic, missional, and pastoral task. Consequently, states Tomlinson, 'When this is in perfect operation God will no doubt open the window of heaven and pour out such a blessing that it will be like Ezekiel's river – a river to swim in'.[41] Here, rather than a soteriological interpretation we find a that Ezekiel 47 is interpreted as a river of blessing that flows in abundance as the members are faithful with their offerings to the church.

The final reference to Ezekiel 47 between the 1906 and 1916 publications is found in the Assemblies of God *Pentecostal Evangel*.[42] Once again, the waters running from the temple are connected to the Holy Spirit. In the article 'The Baptism of the Holy Spirit' H.M. Turney states, 'What is the baptism of the Holy Ghost? It is the flood-tide of spiritual blessing typified by the deep river of Ezekiel's vision'.[43] This blessing from the Holy Spirit, according to Turney was to be understood as an empowerment for service. Interestingly, Turney expands his point by interconnecting the vision of Ezekiel to Luke's accounts found in his gospel (Lk. 24.29) and in Acts 1.8 and to Paul's words in 1 Cor. 3.16 and Eph. 3.17, 18. By so doing, he underscores that as the temple of the Holy Spirit, we are recipients of 'enduement of power for service'.[44]

---

[38] *Church of God General Assembly Minutes*, p. 8.
[39] *Church of God General Assembly Minutes*, p. 8.
[40] *Church of God General Assembly Minutes*, p. 8.
[41] *Church of God General Assembly Minutes*, p. 8.
[42] H.M. Turney, 'The Baptism of the Holy Spirit', *Pentecostal Evangel* 146 (1916), p. 5.
[43] Turney, 'The Baptism of the Holy Spirit', p. 5.
[44] Turney, 'The Baptism of the Holy Spirit', p. 5.

Having looked at some cases of early Pentecostal treatments of Ezekiel 47, I will share a contemporary reading of Ezekiel before sharing mine. This one comes from Pentecostal scholar Rebecca Basdeo Hill. Though her work looks at Ezekiel in its entirety, I will only focus on her treatment of the vision of the water running from the temple.

Basdeo Hill begins her treatment of this section by paying attention to the wording used to describe the flow of water that ran from the threshold. The 'water was *trickling* from the southside' (v. 1). According to Basdeo Hill, the word trickling describes a 'flow of water that is poured out from the aperture of a small bottle'.[45] This will be a crucial point as the reader/hearer moves through the narrative. As we all know, before the prophet stands at the bank, the water has expanded and deepened so much, that Basdeo Hill asserts, because he was 'unable to cross the river, the guide leads Ezekiel back to the river's shore and directs Ezekiel's attention to the banks of the river, which is fringed by a diverse profusion of lush trees'.[46]

Like the guide with the prophet, Basdeo Hill then takes us to the banks and highlights important elements of the text. First, the trees along the bank are many and these 'produce fruit every month, and their evergreen leaves possess healing virtues'.[47] This underscores the themes of 'abundance, fruitfulness, and healing'.[48] Second, Basdeo Hill keeps the intricate connection between what the prophet has seen and the source of the river. She points out that these three properties found in the river are possible because the 'waters flow directly from the sanctuary'.[49] Third, she raises awareness of the all-encompassing reach of the river. In other words, this river goes *everywhere*. Commenting on v. 9, Basdeo Hill states, 'The threefold repetition of the word *kal* ... highlights the comprehensive and far-reaching healing power of the river'.[50] Fourth, in connection to the central theme of her monograph, the healing and restorative promise that we receive from the prophet's vision 'is a direct and necessary correlation of YHWH's glory and holiness'.[51] Here, within this discussion, is

---

[45] Basdeo Hill, *Visions of God in Ezekiel*, p. 143.
[46] Basdeo Hill, *Visions of God in Ezekiel*, p. 143.
[47] Basdeo Hill, *Visions of God in Ezekiel*, p. 143.
[48] Basdeo Hill, *Visions of God in Ezekiel*, p. 143.
[49] Basdeo Hill, *Visions of God in Ezekiel*, p. 143.
[50] Basdeo Hill, *Visions of God in Ezekiel*, p. 143.
[51] Basdeo Hill, *Visions of God in Ezekiel*, p. 144.

where Basdeo Hill makes a key interpretive comment that is central to this study. Though there are no direct mentions of the Holy Spirit in this vision, Basdeo Hill understands that 'there seems to be a firm indication that the river Ezekiel sees flowing from the temple is a representation of YHWH's *ruach*'.[52] This relationship is predicated, for example, upon previous visions of the prophet (see 37 and 39.29).[53] Hence, Basdeo Hill concludes that 'the river flowing from the temple may be another expression of the life-giving presence of YHWH',[54] specifically, the Lord's Spirit. A final point that Basdeo Hill raises, in connection to the previous point of the far-reaching scope of the river, is that this movable glory of YHWH is not confined to God's chosen nation, but it has a broader scope in its mission, that is, the world. In words of Basdeo Hill,

> the meticulous preparation of YHWH's holy place is intended to allow YHWH's soteriological gifts of healing, life, and salvation to flow out of the temple, emphasizing the world's ... immediate access to YHWH's soteriological benefits ... through the giving of the Spirit.[55]

The Living Ecclesiology of Ezekiel 47.1-12

After a long tour which begins in chapter 40, the prophet is taken back to 'the door of the house' (47.1). Interestingly, according to the writer, during this third visit to the door (the previous two found in Ezek. 41.2 and 41.23–25), something got the prophet's attention. The text says, 'and behold, water was flowing from under the threshold of the house' (Ezek. 47.1). The writer's use of the Hebrew word '*hinneh*' (הנה) is of great importance.

'*Hinneh*' (הנה) occurs almost one thousand times in the Old Testament, and the majority of the instances are translated as 'behold'. Grammatically, the term denotes '[a]n interjection demanding attention ..., mainly used to emphasize the information which follows it'.[56]

[52] Basdeo Hill, *Visions of God in Ezekiel*, p. 144.

[53] Looking at these previous connections, Basdeo Hill affirms, 'In other parts of Ezekiel, YHWH's presence that brings about healing and life is expressed through YHWH's *ruach*'. See, Basdeo Hill, *Visions of God in Ezekiel*, p. 144.

[54] Basdeo Hill, *Visions of God in Ezekiel*, p. 144.

[55] Basdeo Hill, *Visions of God in Ezekiel*, pp. 144–45.

[56] Carl Philip Weber, '510 הן' in R. Laird Harris, Gleason L. Archer Jr., and Bruce K. Waltke (eds.), *Theological Wordbook of the Old Testament* (Chicago, IL: Moody Publishers, rev. edn, 2003), p. 220.

Yet of the three times Ezekiel is taken to the door, 'behold' is only used during his last visit (Ezek. 47.1). There are at least two possible scenarios that can be raised. One, there was water flowing and he had not paid attention to it during the first two visits. This is possible; there are many examples in the Bible where people are *unable* to see that which is in plain sight (2 Kgs 6.17; Mk 8.24; Lk. 24.31). The second scenario points to the possibility that there was no water flowing from the door until the third visit. Though I appreciate the possibility of the first scenario, the second seems more likely. Rather than being an event that underscored Ezekiel's lack of faith or his inability to pay attention and see something that he missed, I understand the use of *behold* during his third visit to point to something that is new. It functions as an important transitional phrase, an important moment within the vision.

It is important to highlight that this door is not a typical door. Jerusalem had many doors (Neh. 7.3). However, this door is of the dwelling house of God, the door of God's temple. It is from this door that Ezekiel sees the water flowing. What is noteworthy about this is the reverse use, at least in my mind, of the image of the door. When we think of the temple's door, we usually connect it to the idea of walking *in*. We want people to walk into the church; so, to a certain extent we need people walking *in*. However, this image of the door and the flow of the water as described in Ezekiel reverses the image of walking *in*to that of walking *out*. The importance of this reversal is that it recovers an image of the door that has been lost, especially in contemporary church life. In our everyday language, to walk *out* on someone or from some place is understood as treason, rejection, or putting an end to something. Unfortunately, church language has adopted such an understanding of walking *out*. Back home, when someone has stopped going to church or has stopped believing in Jesus, we use the phrase, *se fue de la iglesia*. Though it literally means 'she or he left the church', the meaning of the phrase is that they walked *out* on us. Thus, to walk *out* is not a good practice but, on the contrary, is understood as something negative (cf. 1 Jn 2.19).

In this passage, the going out has important implications (Ezek. 47.8–12). In the words of Samuel Pagán, 'it highlights the return to an ideal environment of society, where harmony, peace, well-being, safety and health are freely manifested'.[57] However, at first, Ezekiel cannot see the goodness that is produced by the waters that are flowing out. What he sees is a small amount of water, which begs the question, what good could such little water bring? Nevertheless, Ezekiel's guide (40.3) takes him to the bank of the river (47.6),[58] and '*behold*, on the bank of the river there were very many trees on the one side and on the other' (47.7, italics added). Just as he was astonished by the waters flowing from the door of the temple, Ezekiel is amazed at the life and fruitfulness of the small stream that has now become a great body of water. In v. 8 there is an interesting play on words that makes us reevaluate the relationship between walking *in* and walking *out* in our Christian life. Indeed, vv. 1 and 8 establish that the water is flowing out from the door of the temple. Nonetheless, simultaneously, as the waters are flowing *out*, they are also flowing *in*. The passages states, 'These waters go *out*' but also, they 'go down *into* the Arabah' and 'into the sea' (47.8, italics added). As these waters move out of the temple, they are also moving into the city, and take with them a promise of restoration.

What is important to remember at this juncture is that such restoration is a possibility because the waters are flowing from the temple. Interestingly, 'the further they go … their restorative capacity expands, their life-giving power increases'.[59] Yet, although the body of water has moved out, deepened, and widened, the source is still the same; the water flowing from the door of the temple. Thus, what Ezekiel is about to see is the product of the little stream he saw. According to the text, Ezekiel saw trees growing on each side of the river bank (v. 7, 12). He saw refreshed seas (v. 8), life and abundance (v. 9), constant sustenance (v. 10), the preservation of what needed to stay as it was (v. 11), and healing for everything (v. 12). Such act of love, does not go hidden, as Pagán states, 'all is happening within the city, for its blessing'.[60]

Such a vision should make us think about what kind of relationship there is between what we do in church and what kind of impact

---

[57] Samuel Pagán, *Ezequiel y Daniel* (Minneapolis, MN: Augsburg Fortress, 2010), p. 115. Translations from this book are my own.

[58] Notice the change in the description of the water, from a stream of water to a river.

[59] Pagán, *Ezequiel y Daniel*, p. 115.

[60] Pagán, *Ezequiel y Daniel*, p. 115.

it has in our communities. What kind of water is flowing from the door threshold of our temples?

Conclusion

In this chapter, I have offered a Latino Pentecostal reading of Ezek. 47.1-13. In my view, the vision of the prophet serves as a foundational biblical text for the construction of a lived ecclesiology. The chapter began by describing a Latino Pentecostal hermeneutic. Then, it examined examples of how early and contemporary Pentecostals have treated the text. Finally, the chapter ended with my reading of the vision. Now, before moving on to the following chapter, let me share the contributions that surfaced from the hermeneutical community referenced above.

What can we glimpse from these early Pentecostal interpretations of Ezek. 47.1-12 that can contribute to the study at hand? First, according to their interpretation there is some sort of correlation between the waters flowing from the temple and the Holy Spirit. Hence, they understand that the Spirit is at work in the vision. Second, the work of the Spirit is unbounded – in terms of spatiality and spirituality. That is, it has ecclesial and societal implications.[61] Third the waters running from the temple are for both empowerment and service. In other words, there is an interplay between Spirit baptism and *missio Dei*.

Furthermore, what are some important points raised by Basdeo Hill that central to this study? First, everything flows from God's temple. This raises a crucial ecclesiological question that needs consideration. Second, though the source of the waters is the temple, it is not contained by it. It is not only for those who worship in the temple, but it flows into the *polis* and beyond. It goes everywhere, or at least beyond the sight of the prophet. Third, this river brings with it abundance, healing, and life. In other words, it raises the question of salvation. Finally, this river is an expression of the life-giving work of the Holy Spirit.

As stated in the previous chapter, I grew up with an integrative Pentecostal experience. At the beginning of this chapter it was stated

---

[61] Though it is important to recognize that the former gets more attention than the latter.

that Pentecostals overlay their stories on the lived stories found in the biblical narrative. Such interconnection creates expectancy that something similar could happen here and now.[62] Hence, my reading of Ezekiel seeks to give us a glimpse into what type of impact a local church can have when its ecclesiology is aware of the community where she is located. My concern is not whether there is water flowing from our temples: there is water flowing as congregants *flow* in and out of their local churches. I am concerned with how beliefs inform congregants and how these beliefs are embodied in the city. Therefore, in light of this conversation, we can affirm the connection between what happens in *el culto* (the worship service) and our lived spaces. Moving out from the temple, according to Ezekiel's vision, has deep missiological implications. Thus, as we move out from the house of God, we enter our cities and take with us the responsibility of embodying transformation.

---

[62] Lee Roy Martin (ed.), *Pentecostal Hermeneutics: A Reader* (Leiden: Brill, 2013), p. 7.

3

LATIN AMERICAN PENTECOSTAL THEOLOGIES AS LIVED THEOLOGIES

Latin American Testimonies

Pentecostal theology and spirituality happen! They are continually practiced and reflected upon in light of the contexts where they are experienced. The understanding of Pentecostalism as a lived religion relies on the analysis of Pentecostal literature and praxis. Hence, this chapter looks at the former, the literary contributions of Pentecostals regarding the dialogue between the church and the public space. Such an endeavor will not only describe how Pentecostals have approached the topic but will also reveal themes that will be evaluated later (Chapter 5) in relation to the ethnographic findings of the case study (Chapter 4).

Accordingly, this chapter analyzes how Pentecostals are theologizing about the nature and life of the church and how these views inform the public engagement of Pentecostals. This chapter specifically looks at the work of three Latin American theologians who represent three distinct classical Pentecostal denominations and model an integral character of Pentecostal theology and praxis. Furthermore, these voices offer distinct contextual expressions as they are representative of the Spanish speaking Caribbean Latinos, as well as those in the US and Latin America.[1] They are Agustina Luvis Núñez, Eldin Villafañe, and Darío López Rodríguez.

Pentecostals, the Church, and the Public Space

Agustina Luvis Núñez: Pentecostal Equality

Agustina Luvis Núñez is a trained systematic theologian self-described as an Afro-Latina Pentecostal woman. Moreover, she is an ordained minister of the *Iglesia Defensores de la Fe*, an indigenous Pentecostal denomination founded in Puerto Rico. Much of her work is informed by her experiences as a woman that was raised in her loved hometown of Loíza, Puerto Rico. Of all the towns on the island, Loíza is not only the poorest but also has the largest African-descent community. These lived realities are central in her theology. Furthermore, Luvis is associate professor and director of the doctoral program at the *Seminario Evangélico* in Río Piedras, PR and is the founder and coordinator of the Gender, Women, and Justice Pastoral Coalition.

Luvis' work is concerned with Pentecostal ecclesiology and gender. Such work benefits from a rich dialogue between three loci: Pentecostal, Latin American, and feminist theologies. In all, Luvis' aim is to propose 'a more inclusive, ecumenical, ecological, contextual, healing and transformative community'.[2] According to her, this is not only her aim but also her 'definition of what a community of the Spirit stands for'.[3] Echoing the words of Harvey Cox, she also adds

---

[1] This study focuses primarily on Latin American Pentecostal ecclesiologies. This decision is founded upon the following two interconnected premises. The first is the importance of hearing ecclesial contributions from the Majority World, in this case the Latin American Pentecostal voice. Second, I would like to avoid duplication as much as possible. There are already a number of well-written articles that provide an overview of North American and European Pentecostal ecclesiologies. See, for example, Peter Althouse, 'Towards a Pentecostal Ecclesiology: Participation in the Missional Life of the Triune God', *Journal of Pentecostal Theology* 18.2 (September 2009), pp. 230–45; Cartledge, 'Renewal Ecclesiology in Empirical Perspective', *Pneuma* 36 (2014), pp. 5–24.

[2] Agustina Luvis Núñez, 'Sewing a New Cloth: A Proposal for a Pentecostal Ecclesiology Fashioned as a Community Gifted by the Spirit with the Marks of the Church from a Latina Perspective' (PhD diss., Lutheran School of Theology, 2009), p. 5.

[3] Luvis, 'Sewing a New Cloth', p. 5.

that the stream of Pentecostalism birthed in Los Angeles[4] 'erupted among society's disenfranchised, and it envisioned a human community restored by the power of the Spirit'.[5] As a result, the fire of Pentecost gave them hope and became the source of transformation and liberation.[6]

Furthermore, Luvis understands that her view of the church is intrinsically connected to the locus of the community and the theologian's experience. Each voice represented in her – Pentecostal, feminist, and Latino/a – interprets what it means to be the church according to its concrete realities – personal and communal – and from these descriptions emerge. Luvis recognizes that her Caribbean Latina Pentecostal experience shapes her point of view. For her, any attempt to construct a theology rooted in/from the Caribbean soil must take into consideration various essential elements that are contingent to her social construction of reality. What are Luvis' realities? Below, I will summarize these.

First, it must appropriate the 'mosaic of languages, races, ideologies, cultural heritages, economic organizations, and religious backgrounds' that have shaped the Caribbean social imaginary.[7] By Caribbean social imaginary I mean the way that Luvis imagines and embodies her existence as a Caribbean woman.[8]

Second, Luvis emphasizes (concerning history and context) the importance of recognizing the stamp that colonization from Spain, France, Holland, England, and Denmark has left on Caribbean history.[9] Whether the Caribbeaners like it or not, the reality is that these powers contributed to the multifaceted religious tapestry of the region. However, notwithstanding this assertion, Luvis calls for a theology of exploration and a theology of emancipation. These theological approaches seek to 'reflect critically about the Caribbean

---

[4] Though she knows that there are other birthplaces, Luvis' Pentecostal history is connected to the Azusa Street Revival.

[5] Luvis, 'Sewing a New Cloth', p. 19.

[6] Luvis, 'Sewing a New Cloth', p. 26.

[7] Agustina Luvis Núñez, 'Approaching Caribbean Theology from a Pentecostal Perspective', in Harold D. Hunter and Neil Ormerod (eds.), *The Many Faces of Global Pentecostalism* (Cleveland, TN: CPT Press, 2013), p. 130.

[8] Taylor explains, 'I adopt the term imaginary (i) because my focus is on the way ordinary people "imagine" their social surroundings, and this is often not expressed in theoretical terms, but is carried in images, stories, and legends'. For more on social imaginary, see Taylor, *Modern Social Imaginaries*, p. 23.

[9] Luvis, 'Approaching Caribbean Theology', p. 130.

reality in the light of the Christian faith'.[10] As a result, this approach empowers those in the margins of exploitation to speak about God from their unique experiences.

The third element essential to constructing a theology rooted in the Caribbean is to work with local methods. Regarding method, Luvis says, 'This reality includes an intensive participation in the life of the people, specifically their sufferings. This method requires a radical assessment of the needs of the Caribbean constituency, which is seeking to interpret the meaning of the Gospel in the Caribbean context'.[11] In other words, instead of beginning with perennial questions, Caribbean theology is rooted in the concrete realities of the people and communities. In other words, it is anthropological. According to Luvis, her goal 'is to help Caribbean people understand their situation in order to change it through a process of reflection and action'.[12] Such an aim advocates for a shift from the imposition of colonial hermeneutics to an understanding that God dwells among the Caribbean islands and can be approached through Caribbean expressions.[13]

Luvis and Pentecostal Ecclesiology

Luvis' goal is to propose an egalitarian Pentecostal ecclesiology: in other words, a 'church where the image of God as female and male is affirmed'[14] and where both 'work hand in hand for liberation and justice'.[15] How does this happen? What are Luvis' ecclesial contributions?

Drinking from her own well,[16] Luvis rejoices in her *Loiceña* experience (this is how Puerto Ricans refer to people from the town of

---

[10] Luvis, 'Approaching Caribbean Theology', p. 131.

[11] Luvis, 'Approaching Caribbean Theology', p. 132.

[12] Luvis, 'Approaching Caribbean Theology', p. 133.

[13] Luvis understands that Caribbean theology is far from emancipation, but it is on the right track. Yet it can cover more ground by 'working dialectically in each Caribbean country independently and as a unique region of communities as a whole'. Luvis, 'Approaching Caribbean Theology', p. 133.

[14] Agustina Luvis Núñez, *Creada a su imagen: Ministerio Series AETH: Una pastoral integral para la mujer* (Nashville: Abingdon Press, 2012), Kindle, 262-65, chapter 2, section 1. My translation.

[15] Luvis, *Creada a su imagen*, Kindle loc. 73–75, chapter 1, section 1. My translation.

[16] The idea is that she considers her context and realities as a locus for constructing her theological argument. For a thorough explanation of this concept, see Gustavo Gutiérrez, *We Drink from Our Own Wells: The Spiritual Journey of a People* (Maryknoll, NY: Orbis Books, 20th anniv. edn, 2003).

Loíza) and draws strength from such experiences and cultural richness. As a matter of fact, her view of the church is consonant with *Las fiestas de Santiago Apóstol.*[17] She describes this feast as one that characterizes the African flavor of Puerto Ricans, a feast that celebrates 'common roots, promotes the sense of community, and offers a space to share the stories of those who [return] to visit their town'.[18] The importance of this feast lies in that 'there is a marked tendency in the history of Puerto Rico's popular feasts to appropriate some religious spaces within our own autochthonous context and in this way to evidence their no-strangeness'.[19] Consequently, for Puerto Ricans (not only *Loiceños*), there is some overlapping between the sacred and the public. Luvis acknowledges that this connection 'shaped [her] vision of what the church must be'.[20] Consequently, Luvis sees the church as an intertwined divine-human event. Such an understanding of the church calls for a community that prophesies to and redeems the cultural, political, and economic realms through its liturgy. Therefore, 'The church is like Loíza's popular feast'.[21]

In her assessment of the relationship between God and the Caribbean, Luvis affirms that the church cannot portray God as a foreigner. To do so is to speak about a God that is not capable of responding to the realities and issues of the Caribbean region.[22] For too long God was seen as a 'pilgrim' in the Caribbean Christian landscape. However, through the development of local methodology, voices, and goals, Caribbean theology has underscored the importance of the 'indigenizing principle'.[23] Regarding this point, Luvis implies that in the same way that Caribbean theology has benefited

---

[17] A popular festival celebrated every year on July 25. For a description of *Las fiestas de Santiago Apóstol,* see Ricardo Alegría, 'The Fiesta of Santiago Apóstol (St. James the Apostle) in Loíza, Puerto Rico', *The Journal of American Folklore* 69.272 (Apr.–Jun. 1956), pp. 123–34.

[18] Luvis, 'Approaching Caribbean Theology', p. 129.

[19] Luvis, 'Approaching Caribbean Theology', p. 129.

[20] Reflecting on this point, Luvis mentions that her parents affirmed in her and her sister both their *Loiceño* and Pentecostal identity. She adds that 'they saw no contradiction to affirm both traditions in our lives'. Moreover, Luvis affirms her parents' position by underscoring the African roots of Pentecostal spirituality. Luvis, 'Approaching Caribbean Theology', p. 129.

[21] Luvis, 'Sewing a New Cloth', p. 157.

[22] Luvis, 'Sewing a New Cloth', p. 162.

[23] For an explanation of the indigenizing and pilgrim principles, see Andrew F. Walls, *The Missionary Movement in Christian History: Studies in the Transmission of Faith* (Maryknoll, NY: Orbis Books, 1996), pp. 7–9.

by local and indigenous contributions, the church must not be foreign to women, and women must be given (or reclaim) their space in defining the church in their own words and through their concrete realities. Though there has been some progress in this regard, there is much work left to be done.

Furthermore, Caribbean theology, as a theology in context, must critically wrestle with the particularities of culture.[24] As Lesslie Newbigin says, 'True contextualization accords the gospel its rightful primacy, its power to penetrate every culture and speak within each culture, in its own speech and symbol, the word which is both No and Yes, both judgment and grace'.[25] Luvis espouses Newbigin's premise, affirming that the 'process of emancipation, decolonization and liberation must be part of the church agenda, specifically in the Pentecostal church, in accordance with the strong claim of liberation'.[26] Thus, for her, the church is not only speaking of matters of faith but also of life. To my understanding, there is no way to bifurcate these two within the Latin American context.

Additionally, Luvis attempts to propose an egalitarian Pentecostal ecclesiology. This point stands as the heart of her argument. Ecclesiology, she cries out, suffers when women are silent. Luvis emphatically states, 'A church governed by men is more than a heresy; it is a stumbling block for the construction of a more egalitarian society'.[27] Therefore, her ecclesiological proposal is constructed through the voices of women who are willing to theologize about the church. In the end, Luvis explains that in light of their conversations, these women see the church as a Spirit-filled community which by the leading of the Holy Spirit is responsible to preach the gospel to all is equal forms.[28] However, this does not happen until, according to Luvis, we 'recognize the signs of the times … and recover the spaces

---

[24] Mercedes, one of Luvis' interviewees, highlights the need for the church to look into the cultural realm. She states, 'The Pentecostal church must continue to take seriously, as it did in the beginnings, the socio-cultural reality of the people and to make it a central part of its vision and mission'. Luvis, 'Sewing a New Cloth', p. 170.

[25] Lesslie Newbigin, *The Gospel in a Pluralist Society* (Grand Rapids, MI: Eerdmans, 1989), p. 152.

[26] Luvis, 'Sewing a New Cloth', p. 163.

[27] Luvis, 'Sewing a New Cloth', p. 187.

[28] Luvis, 'Sewing a New Cloth', p. 179.

of life, assuming a critical attitude toward those who cause death and dehumanization of the other'.[29]

All of this brings Luvis to her working definition of the church. She states, 'There is no doubt that to be church, in the Pentecostal milieu, is to be a fellowship gifted by the Spirit [and] to [bear] witness [of] Jesus Christ's gospel to the world'.[30] She also adds that this giftedness 'must be focused on the restoration of the egalitarian principles'.[31] In this definition, we can see the wholistic or integral nature of her theology. Luvis' understanding of the church is both theological and missional (practical). On the one hand, the church is a 'fellowship gifted by the Holy Spirit'. Such fellowship can happen if those who participate, both male and female, are equal recipients of the *charismata*. By equal, Luvis does not mean that all receive the same gift but that, regardless of the gifts,[32] the Agent is the same and, thus, there is equal participation in the Spirit. On the other hand, Luvis underscores the missiological implications for the church. Whatever the gifts given to the community; they are given for the testimony of Christ to the world. If my understanding of Luvis is correct, declaring that the community is baptized with and in the Spirit is not enough; the world needs to witness and be the recipient of the Spirit's work in the church.

Luvis not only presents her definition but also states how this form of being church is modeled. In her assessment, to be this kind of community 'requires attention to the specific context rather than working with generic models'.[33] As stated in the previous section, the being of church is a divine-human event. It is initiated by the triune God but is embodied by us. But this 'us' is not isolated from the locus. Luvis adds, 'We need to be guided by the Spirit and also be attentive to the signs of the times and spaces …, [to] take into consideration the historical, social, cultural, economic and religious elements that

---

[29] Luvis, 'Sewing a New Cloth', p. 179.
[30] Luvis, 'Sewing a New Cloth', p. 183.
[31] Luvis, 'Sewing a New Cloth', p. 183.
[32] Regarding the gifts of the Spirit, Luvis states, 'I note a broader understanding of the gifts of the Spirit and an expanded list of charisms. According to these women, the gifts of the Spirit are not limited to those traditionally identified by Paul (1 Cor. 14). They take that catalogue as representative rather than exhaustive'. Luvis, 'Sewing a New Cloth', p. 181.
[33] Luvis, 'Sewing a New Cloth', p. 183.

shape our reality'.[34] In short, we are called to embody a church that engages the world and listens to its needs.

Contributions for a Lived Ecclesiology

Although Luvis' goal is to articulate a Caribbean (Puerto Rican) Pentecostal ecclesiology that takes seriously the contribution of women, her study has interesting ramifications for the question of the church and public engagement. What follows are some of the findings that surface from my reading of Luvis' work.[35]

Luvis emphasizes that the church needs a keen understanding of its cultural landscape. In *Creada a su imagen* (Created in His Image), Luvis reflects on various encounters that Jesus had with women throughout his ministry. Commenting on the encounter between Jesus and the Syrophoenician woman, she states, 'This woman challenges Him to recognize that personal and communal life can be enriched when we open space for perspectives, voices, eyes, and interpretations that come from people that are excluded, silenced, or invisible'.[36] Elsewhere she also affirms, 'The Pentecostal church must continue to take seriously, as it did in the beginnings, the socio-cultural reality of the people and to make it a central part of its vision and mission'.[37] Both quotes raise the question of the particularity and the universality of the gospel. Thus, to develop an ecclesiology that seriously engages the public, it is necessary to see beyond ourselves and also have a sense beyond our space.[38] Such an approach recognizes the fluid overlapping of the church and the public space.

Another point that is helpful in Luvis' argument is the need to become visible within society. In other words, it is not enough to have a keen understanding of the cultural landscape. The church must

---

[34] Luvis, 'Sewing a New Cloth', p. 183.

[35] It is no surprise that much of this section comes from the ethnographic interviews and testimonies that Luvis has gathered over several years. These women, according to Luvis, live between the worshiping community and the concrete realities of their society. Luvis, 'Sewing a New Cloth', p. 169.

[36] Luvis, *Creada a su imagen*, Kindle, 170-72, chapter 1, section 2. My translation.

[37] Luvis, 'Sewing a New Cloth', p. 170.

[38] Commenting on this double movement, in light of the priestly character of the people of God, Christopher Wright says, 'This dual movement ... (from God to the people and from the people to God) is reflected in prophetic visions concerning the nations, which included both *centrifugal* and *centripetal* dynamics. There would be a going out from God and coming in to God'. Christopher J.H. Wright, *The Mission of God: Unlocking the Bible's Grand Narrative* (Downer's Grove, IL: IVP Academic, 2006), p. 331. Emphasis added.

become visible in the realities of its context. One of the women Luvis interviewed said that the Pentecostal church 'should be more visible in social, ethical, ecological, political and economic struggles'.[39] Knowing the signs of our times is futile if the church does not act and become ever-present in the midst of the needs of society. For Luvis, to become visible is more than knowing, we are responsible for speaking and acting out. We cannot have one without the other. On the one hand, the church needs to 'publicly manifest itself against all forms of violence against human beings. Violence is sinful because it ignores the image of God in humans.'[40] However, Luvis understands that active participation needs to occur with sound judgment.[41] On the other hand, 'The church has to act with the conviction that she is embodying *concrete* ways of understanding [the] love for justice'.[42] Interestingly, such a practice is guided by the church's spiritual disciplines. Here Luvis speaks specifically of intercession. For example, as the church engages in public action, she is also called 'to intercede through prayer'.[43] But this prayer, states Luvis, is 'not only for the spiritual needs of people but for the social, economic realms as well'.[44]

Finally, Luvis makes a clear connection between the Spirit-filled community and the public responsibilities that are at play. The following quote expresses this idea:

> For the Pentecostal church '*está prohibido olvidar*' ([it] is forbidden to forget) that the significant socio-reality in the beginning and development of Pentecostalism was its ministry among the 'disinherited', the socially marginalized, ethnically heterogeneous, struggling working classes and impoverished unemployed people. To be Pentecostal is not only to articulate a theology that corresponds with the community's reality. It is also to concretize this reflection in a praxis that affirms the grace of being gifted.[45]

---

[39] Luvis, 'Sewing a New Cloth', p. 170.
[40] Luvis, *Creada a su imagen*, Kindle, 546-47, chapter 3, section 2.
[41] Luvis, 'Sewing a New Cloth', p. 173.
[42] Luvis, 'Sewing a New Cloth', p. 172.
[43] Luvis, 'Sewing a New Cloth', p. 174.
[44] Luvis, 'Sewing a New Cloth', p. 175.
[45] Luvis, 'Sewing a New Cloth', p. 184.

In other words, for Luvis, the public nature of the Pentecostal community has been present since the early life of Pentecostalism.[46] Such a critical commitment, rather than being something foreign, is part of its identity.

Eldin Villafañe: Pentecostals and Social Justice

Eldin Villafañe was born in Puerto Rico but he has lived, studied, taught, and ministered within the Latino/a context in the United States. He is a credentialed minister of the Assemblies of God (AG) and has served as a local church educator and as an AG executive. Furthermore, Villafañe was the founder and director of Gordon-Conwell's Center for Urban Ministerial Education (CUME). Villafañe has dedicated his life to urban centers and to the development and embodiment of what he calls a Spirit-ethic approach. For Villafañe, this Spirit-ethic needs to be embodied by the local church. In other words, it is a commitment of the Christian community to its local community. Hence, he states, 'churches that are not concerned with the city and the urban spaces are churches that have lost their vision'.[47]

Villafañe points out three theological motifs that need to (re)surface in a Latino/a Pentecostal church, if she is willing to embody a Spirit-filled ethic. That is, the missionary commitment with the poor, ecclesiological contextualization, and the comprehension of the spiritual life of the church. For Villafañe, the Pentecostal church must affirm her 'missionary commitment with the poor'.[48] Villafañe understands that such a commitment has been part of Pentecostalism since its early history, and more so among Latinas/os. Also, the Spirit-filled community must seek 'ecclesiological contextualization in every dimension: geographical, physical, etc'.[49] This motif underscores an integral approach to contextualization and a dual understanding of the locus. On the one hand, the gospel must be translatable into local forms. On the other hand, this call to contextualization is an appeal for the church to be sensitive to the societal context in which she is

---

[46] If not the first, Walter Hollenweger is one of the first Pentecostal scholars to affirm this 'critical' stream of Pentecostalism. See Hollenweger, *Pentecostalism*, pp. 204–17.

[47] Eldin Villafañe, *Seek the Peace of the City: Reflections on Urban Ministry* (Grand Rapids, MI: Eerdmans Publishing Company, 1995), p. 2.

[48] Eldin Villafañe, *El Espíritu liberador: Hacia una ética social pentecostal hispanoamericana* (Buenos Aires: Nueva Creación, 1996), p. 113. My translation.

[49] Villafañe, *El Espíritu Liberador*, p. 113. My translation.

established. Finally, the church needs to emphasize the 'comprehension of the spiritual life of the church, which is not limited by the aesthetic of the building or its surroundings'.[50] In other words, though there is an intrinsic connection between *el culto* (worship service) and the community, the *locus theologicus* of Pentecostalism stems from what takes place in *el culto*.

From the start, Villafañe's Spirit-ethic is intrinsically connected to the life and mission of the church. Therefore, in the following section, Villafañe's ecclesial contributions will be further developed.

Villafañe and Pentecostal Ecclesiology

The Spirit-filled church has an irrefutable responsibility to make herself present through word and deeds. The biblical witness, according to Villafañe, calls for both a 'vertical focus … and a horizontal focus … Both approaches can only be fulfilled in the power of the Spirit'.[51] However, Villafañe recognizes that the latter – the horizontal focus – sometimes is lacking within Latino/a Pentecostalism. 'This should become a challenge for Latino/a Pentecostal churches, that they finally recognize that a relevant and true spirituality must be integral and must respond equally to the vertical and to the horizontal dimension'.[52] With this challenge in mind, let us look at Villafañe's proposals.

Villafañe's Spirit-ethic is rooted in the church's faculty to *love* and in the ability, she has to incarnate her love in *social actions*. Certainly, love is the main motivation for Jesus' compassion and mercy. 'The life and the cross of Jesus must become our model for reaching others and the depth of our love.'[53] Thus, our love for others is fully expressed through the sacrifice of our self for the sake of those in need. 'The social importance of love can be manifested in various

---

[50] Villafañe, *El Espíritu Liberador*, p. 113. My translation.

[51] Villafañe, *El Espíritu Liberador*, p. 147. My translation.

[52] This challenge toward the vertical dimension is a call to 'participate in God's kingdom … It is to take seriously God's call to the church to become a community of the Spirit *in* the world and *for* the world, but *not* as part of the world'. Villafañe commends the Latino/a Pentecostal church for her evangelistic and missionary efforts throughout the world; yet he also asserts that 'the prophetic voice … against sinful structures and in favor of social justice has been absent'. Thus, Villafañe underscores the gap between what happens in the worship service and what happens after. 'The Spirit is present in the service … but the missionary focus … is absent'. Villafañe, *El Espíritu Liberador*, pp. 149, 169, 174–75. My translation.

[53] Villafañe, *El Espíritu Liberador*, p. 182. My translation.

ways, one of which is through the development of human rights.'[54] If there is a connection between love and the development of human rights, it is indispensable to maintain the interrelatedness of love and justice. This interrelatedness can serve as an answer to the present bifurcation between vertical and horizontal worship. Equally important, Villafañe mentions, 'When justice is perceived as an expression of love, it makes the engagement feasible for everyone'.[55]

Similar to Luvis, Villafañe's proposal challenges the Pentecostal church to understand her nature. The church needs to look into Scripture, look back to tradition, and yield to the Spirit. If we do this, we can identify four early church practices that were central for the post-Pentecost community. These marks are *koinonia*, *leitourgia*, *kerigma,* and *diakonia.* I will briefly explain his argument.

For Villafañe, the church is the community of the Spirit. It is within the locus of the church where the truest expression of *koinonia* must be embodied. Because the church is the community of the Spirit, 'its advancement in the world relies on its ability to live according to its nature'.[56] If the church is the truest expression of Christ, and Christ is God with us, then the same communal nature that exists within the triune God must be manifested in the church.[57]

Furthermore, Villafañe makes a powerful statement on what he means by *leitourgia.* This is not just singing, reading, and preaching, but *leitourgia* is also concerned with the church's social responsibility.[58] Consequently, 'there is a profound spiritual relation between service (social justice) and empathy with the oppressed and authentic worship'.[59] In addition, Latino/a Pentecostals have demonstrated at times a narrow understanding of the proclamation of the gospel. As a consequence, Pentecostals have overshadowed the prophetic character

---

[54] Villafañe, *El Espíritu Liberador,* p. 182. My translation.

[55] Villafañe, *El Espíritu Liberador,* p. 183. My translation.

[56] Villafañe, *El Espíritu Liberador,* p. 185. My translation.

[57] For example, Zizioulas states, 'The being of God is a relational being: without the concept of communion it would not be possible to speak of the being of God … It would be unthinkable to speak of the "one God" before speaking of the God who is communion … the Holy Trinity'. As God's image bearer, the human subject shares not the ontological nature of the triune God but his relational nature. Thus, human beings are social beings. We were created with the need to live in communion. See John D. Zizioulas, *Being as Communion: Studies in Personhood and the Church* (Crestwood, NY: St. Vladimir's Seminary, 1997), p. 17.

[58] This statement raises the question of *el culto* outside of *el culto.*

[59] Villafañe, *El Espíritu liberador,* p. 187. My translation.

of our spirituality, becoming self-centered in our *kerigma*, that is preaching to herself, and avoid preaching, for example, against social oppression and other public matters. Villafañe asserts, 'as long as the Hispanic Pentecostal church discovers the reach and depth of the *kerigma*, its members will unite with others and bear witness in the face of the many evils besetting the *barrios* and the world'.[60] He concludes by challenging the Latino/a Pentecostal church, saying that the church, though not of this world, is at the service of it.[61] Therefore, if we are to express faithful *diakonia* – that is serving other in words and deeds – 'it cannot only focus on conversion or on the well-being of church members, but its truest expression of love and of the gospel is embodied by serving a suffering humanity'.[62]

Elsewhere, Villafañe expands on the marks mentioned above and affirms that Christian theology is called to be *sierva*, *santificadora*, and *sanadora*.[63] He begins his argument by stating that our identity as Christians is rooted in who Christ is, rather than in the vocation that he has called us to live. Thus, if theological education must be rooted in Christ, then Christ's mission becomes our self-understanding. In other words, theology 'is *la sierva* (servant) of the poor and the oppressed'. A *sierva* approach calls for a theology that stands in *solidaridad* (solidarity) with 'the struggles and the joys of the people'[64] and becomes an agent that liberates. Moreover, Christian theology as a sanctifying agent reaffirms the prophetic character of theology.

For Villafañe, a theology that is *santificadora* (sanctifying) is called to 'separate and denunciate all *pecado* (sin) y *mal* (evil)'.[65] Another interesting point within this discussion of theology as *santificadora* is Villafañe's understanding of theology as a 'political act'.[66] He states, we should 'be more clear and intentional in terms of whose benefit is accrued by its production … As such, scholarship as *Santificadora* blows the cover off the myth of nonpolitical or apolitical scholarship'.[67] In this regard, theology becomes a 'voice for the

---

[60] Villafañe, *El Espíritu Liberador*, p. 188.

[61] Villafañe, *El Espíritu Liberador*, p. 188.

[62] Villafañe, *El Espíritu Liberador*, p. 189.

[63] Servant, sanctifier, and healer. See chapter 3 of Villafañe, *Seek the Peace of the City*.

[64] Villafañe, *Seek the Peace of the City*, p. 8.

[65] Villafañe, *Seek the Peace of the City*, p. 9.

[66] Villafañe, *Seek the Peace of the City*, p. 9.

[67] Villafañe, *Seek the Peace of the City*, p. 9.

voiceless', a 'vital prophetic voice in the barrios', and an agent of liberation.[68] This is how the body of Christ is the church.

Lastly, Christian theology as *sanadora* (healing) underscores the 'being and the doing'[69] of the Christian community in the city. For Villafañe, theology as *sanadora* calls for an active presence, for a committed 'being'. Healing cannot happen if disengagement is the root of the church: to be *sanadora* requires that we be present with our *pueblo*.[70]

The church that is guided by a Spirit-ethic is a church that embodies a wholistic spirituality. On the one hand, Villafañe defines wholistic as an encompassing engagement, one that includes word and deeds.[71] On the other hand, by spirituality he means, 'obedience to God, the following of Jesus in the power of the Spirit'.[72] Thus, wholistic spirituality is the 'following of Jesus in both personal transformation/piety and social transformation/piety'.[73] In sum, Villafañe categorizes churches that seek to live with such orientation as churches that have a healthy tension between 'contemplative and apostolic activity'.[74]

Contributions for a Lived Ecclesiology

Villafañe's reflection on urban ministry is biblically founded on Jeremiah's letter to the exiles in Babylon (Jer. 29.5–7). According to Villafañe, Jeremiah's letter to the exiles in Babylon comes with a vision for God's people *then* and for the church of *today*. Among the important elements that can be raised, Villafañe sustains that Jeremiah's words address important questions such as 'What is the role of the people of God in the city? ... What is the role of the church in the city today?'[75] The answers to these questions (some of these were summarized in the previous section) form what Villafañe calls the Jeremiah Paradigm, a 'wholistic vision for the city'.[76] Unquestionably, Villafañe's Spirit-ethic has many contributions for the church's public

---

[68] Villafañe, *Seek the Peace of the City*, p. 9.
[69] Villafañe, *Seek the Peace of the City*, p. 10.
[70] Villafañe, *Seek the Peace of the City*, pp. 10–11.
[71] Villafañe, *Seek the Peace of the City*, p. 13.
[72] Villafañe, *Seek the Peace of the City*, p. 13.
[73] Villafañe, *Seek the Peace of the City*, p. 13.
[74] Villafañe, *Seek the Peace of the City*, p. 14.
[75] Villafañe, *Seek the Peace of the City*, p. 2.
[76] Villafañe, *Seek the Peace of the City*, p. 2.

presence. In the following paragraphs, I will attempt to tease these out.

In *Seek the Peace of the City*, Villafañe states the following about Christ and the cross, 'The cross of our Lord Jesus Christ is not only a historical reality that is crucial to our theological self-understanding and experience of redemption, but it is also a paradigm – a model – for our lives and for the life of the church – especially if it is to play a redemptive and revitalizing role in the urban world'.[77] For Villafañe, the church, the body of the crucified and risen Lord, has inarguably the responsibility to be a *redemptive* and a *revitalizing* agent. Such responsibility is not fulfilled by reaching the city from afar but by being immersed in it. Though he recognizes that there is room to grow, he also affirms that the Latino/a church has modeled this kind of church in the United States.

The Latino/a church, according to Villafañe, is a model of a *liberated church*. This means a church that is 'providing a community of "freedom", "dignity", "self-worth", "comfort", "strength", "hope", "joy", – "abundant life"'.[78] Hence, the church is a *social service provider*. This element not only underscores the giving of services but also 'advocacy'.[79] Furthermore, this liberated church has always sought to maintain her *cultural survival and affirmation*. As such, the Latino/a Pentecostal community is a 'locus of cultural validation'.[80] It is a place where we (re)discover our culture: a culture-affirming community. In addition, the Latino/a church sees through the lens of the *hermeneutical advantage of the poor*. She exegetes the needs of the community through the perspective of the oppressed and the marginalized. She approaches her theology and praxis through this vantage point. Finally, says Villafañe, the Latino/a church is a *signpost*. The church is a 'prophetic community' or 'priestly community'[81] which speaks to principalities, to other churches, to church members themselves, and to the church herself.

Villafañe emphasizes that a church that 'seeks the peace of the city' needs to develop what he calls a 'burning patience'. A church with a burning patience 'believes that in the "now and not yet" of the

---

[77] Villafañe, *Seek the Peace of the City*, p. 31.
[78] Villafañe, *Seek the Peace of the City*, p. 33.
[79] Villafañe, *Seek the Peace of the City*, pp. 33–34.
[80] Villafañe, *Seek the Peace of the City*, p. 34.
[81] Villafañe, *Seek the Peace of the City*, p. 37.

Kingdom of God, one can believe in a city where there is comprehension and clarity, care and concern, consolation, justice and love. In other words, there can be shalom.'[82] The importance of this statement for the public role of the church lies in that such a commitment does not happen overnight; rather, it is a call to an intentional and patience *acompañamiento* (accompaniment).[83]

Elsewhere, Villafañe has spoken about the politics of the Spirit.[84] His basic premise is the following:

> Freedom/Liberation, not as defined by the liberal and enlightenment heritage, but as biblical promise, is at the heart of the Gospel. The Gospel, in other words, affirms the Liberating Spirit's task in all human encounters with God, and the Liberating Spirit's desire to free from all enslavement – be they moral or spiritual, ecological or ecclesiastical, economic or political. The Gospel affirms the Liberating Spirit's historical project as the great personal and social transformer – and our task is to live out the imperative: as we live in the Spirit, so to walk in the Spirit (Galatians 5.25).[85]

There are various elements here that need to be unpacked. First, Villafañe's definition of freedom is not founded on a popular understanding of freedom, which may be the power to act or think without hindrance; or the self-determination attributed to the will. Contrary to that, he proposes a biblical/theological definition: free from all enslavement. The second interesting element is that the Spirit's work is both historical and transcendental. As a divine being of the Godhead, the Spirit moves *into* and *from* this world freely to fulfill God's salvific mission. A third element found in this quote is that the Spirit's work moves from the person to the community and from the community to the person.

Moreover, Villafañe understands that the Holy Spirit has a political agenda in the world. Going beyond Yoder (and his followers), who believed that the church is the central political institution in a

---

[82] Villafañe, *Seek the Peace of the City*, p. 44.

[83] By *acompañamiento* (accompaniment) I mean a transformative, long-standing commitment. Though it seems at first that what one gives and the other receives, a true act of *acompañamiento* is a two-way street.

[84] This was Villafañe's SPS presidential address. See Eldin Villafañe, 'The Politics of the Spirit: Reflections on a Theology of Social Transformation for the Twenty-First Century', *Pneuma* 18.2 (September 1, 1996), pp. 161–70.

[85] Villafañe, 'The Politics of the Spirit', p. 162.

Christian social ethic, Villafañe sought to expand the map and 'embrace the total social order and its organizing institutions as legitimate arenas for a true and holistic Christian discipleship'.[86] I understand that Villafañe's proposal seems too optimistic and too this-worldly. However, he makes his case by saying that to understand such a proposal 'we need a better understanding of the Spirit's historical project – the Reign of God'.[87] This proposal does not reject the idea of the church as the polis or the 'community of life'. What Villafañe adds, if I am reading him correctly, is the broadening of the reach of the church. Thus, it may be that he is moving our understanding of God's political activity from being church-centered to being creation-centered or kingdom-centered. To understand Villafañe's position, it is important to define what he means by politics. Using Paul Lehmann's definition, he states, 'Politics … is what God is doing in the world to make and to keep human life'.[88] Therefore, no institution is exempt from the divine work and from the active participation of believers. Thus, he summarizes, 'we are involved in politics whenever in society we are concerned about building community – that can be in the neighborhood, at school or work, or in the broader institutions of society, including "state-government" politics'.[89]

Regardless of the central role of the Holy Spirit in his theological argumentation, Villafañe is not oblivious to Christ's role. He affirms that God's reign became manifested with Christ's incarnation and is still present today by the sending of the Spirit and the establishment of the church. 'The Gospel of the Reign of God is the good news that in the life, death, and resurrection of Christ, God's Reign is manifested in the physical and historical affairs of people, now able to experience the Spirit's total liberation.'[90] He also adds, 'We need, though, to always be reminded that while the church is not the Reign of God, yet, as the community of the Spirit – where the Spirit manifest [*sic*] itself in a unique and particular way … it has the high calling

---

[86] Villafañe, 'The Politics of the Spirit', p. 162.
[87] Villafañe, 'The Politics of the Spirit', p. 162.
[88] Paul Lehmann, 'The Foundations and Pattern of Christian Behavior' in John A. Hutchinson (ed.), *Christian Faith and Social Action* (New York: Charles Scribner's Sons, 1953), pp. 94–95.
[89] Villafañe, 'The Politics of the Spirit', pp. 164–65.
[90] Villafañe, 'The Politics of the Spirit', p. 166.

to both reflect and witness to the values of the Reign, by the power of the Spirit to the world'.[91]

In short, for Villafañe, Christians cannot reject and be afraid of the public sphere. Yes, we need to be aware of its corruption and seduction. However, Christians are also called to serve within that realm with the goal of contributing to a healthy community of life, especially when working among displaced and marginalized people.[92] Hence, just as Christ did to those around him, Christians are called to model 'Spirit-lead actions'[93] in this world.

Darío López Rodríguez: Pentecostals and Politics

Darío López, a native Peruvian, is a theologian who presently serves as a local pastor for the Church of God (Cleveland) in Peru. Also, he has served as the Administrative Bishop of the Church of God (Cleveland) in Peru, Faith-Based Consultant for various Peruvian presidents, and as the president of the *Concilio Nacional Evangélico del Perú* (the Peruvian National Evangelical Council). Additionally, he has traveled throughout the Americas teaching and speaking about issues of social justice, the love for the marginalized, and the inherent calling that the church must be a prophetic voice in matters of politics. López's Pentecostal thought in concerned with a spirituality that is centered on the missional work of Christ and seeks to liberate the marginalized, the oppressed, and the underprivileged of this world through the agency of the liberating Spirit of God.[94]

---

[91] Villafañe, 'The Politics of the Spirit', p. 166.

[92] Regarding this, Villafañe states, 'Given the socioeconomic conditions of most Hispanics in the USA, the Hispanic church must develop a theology and social ethic that call for economic and political engagement'. See Villafañe, *Seek the Peace of the City*, p. 73.

[93] Villafañe, 'The Politics of the Spirit', p. 168.

[94] Though there are many other important themes within Darío's Pentecostal theology, the themes of Christ's mission, the liberating agency of the Spirit, and the love and service for the downtrodden are found throughout his writings. Darío López, *Pentecostalismo y transformación social* (Buenos Aires: Ediciones Kairós, 2003); Darío López, *La fiesta del Espíritu: Espiritualidad y celebración pentecostal* (Lima, Peru: Ediciones Puma, 2006); Darío López, *Pentecostalismo y misión integral: Teología del Espíritu, teología de la vida* (Lima, Peru: Ediciones Puma, 2008); Darío López, *La propuesta política del reino de Dios: Estudios bíblicos sobre iglesia, sociedad y estado* (Lima, Peru: Ediciones Puma, 2009); Darío López and Richard E. Waldrop, 'The God of Life and the Spirit of Life: The Social and Political Dimension of Life in the Spirit', *Studies in World Christianity* 17 (January 2011), pp. 1–11; Darío López, *The Liberating Mission of Jesus: The Message of the Gospel of Luke* (Pentecostals, Peacemaking, and Social Justice Series; Eugene, OR: Pickwick Publications, 2012); Darío López and Víctor Arroyo, *Tejiendo un nuevo rostro público* (Lima, Peru: Ediciones Puma, 2014).

For López, there is no division between the sacred and the public. By this I do not mean that he has an uncritical stance of the public space. But for him, to proclaim Christ as *Kyrios* of all the *kosmos* has serious public implications. Yet, before unpacking his view regarding the public calling of the church, let me present some of the ecclesial contributions that flow from his Pentecostal theology and spiritualty.

López and Pentecostal Ecclesiology

To appreciate López's thought, it is necessary to understand from *where* he is writing.[95] He writes as a single father who vowed to live simply and pastor who is committed within a community with much need. It is from this locus of life and through his Pentecostal experience that López writes. What follows is a sketch of López's perception of the Pentecostal community in the world.

One of López's central themes is the liberating mission of Jesus. For López, just as God liberated many individuals and called them into his body through the work of Jesus and in the power of the Holy Spirit, the church has an innate calling to continue this mission wherever she is present. In his reading of the third gospel, López sees that Jesus' mission was a challenge to the establishment.

> Jesus' association with individuals who were undervalued and excluded by society also explains the reasons why the representatives of the Jewish society saw the ministry of the Galilean preacher as a permanent threat to their religious interests and their particular political interests.[96]

Reflecting on this, López challenges the church to accept such a role. As a church filled with the Spirit, we have to take 'the daily risk' of being publicly identified with society's needs.[97] This risk, in López's words, is rooted in love. He further explains, 'The special love that God has for the excluded and the scorned constitutes a constant missional challenge for the disciples of the crucified and risen Lord'.[98]

---

[95] Not only in terms of its *locus* but also in terms of his experiences.
[96] López, *The Liberating Mission of Jesus*, p. 20.
[97] López, *The Liberating Mission of Jesus*, p. 22.
[98] López, *The Liberating Mission of Jesus*, p. 24.

Such a liberating mission underscores the need to live as an 'alternative community'.[99] This is how López understands the Pentecostal church in the world. For him, this form of living is intrinsically connected to the Spirit's liberating work. He writes,

> For Pentecostals who have been liberated by the God of life from the chains of oppression which had kept them bowed in subhuman conditions, it should not seem strange to affirm that the defense of the dignity of all human beings, as God's creations, becomes a concrete way of living in the Spirit.[100]

Hence, for López, becoming part of the Pentecostal community does not demand withdrawal from society but, in contrast, a boundary crossing, which entails an engagement with the realities of human society. The Pentecostal community, empowered by the Holy Spirit, is called to be an 'alternative society', a 'countercultural society', and to represent a 'new humanity in Christ'.[101]

Another image or theme that López uses is that of the church as a service provider. In other words, he understands that the church is at the service of her communities. This service is described as sacrificial giving. For López, if the liberated community seeks to present itself as an alternative community, it ought to embody the ethics of God's kingdom, not the ethics of this world. While the ethics of this world affirm such things as taking advantage of others and self-gratification, which are 'clear marks that reject the values of God's kingdom',[102] the ethics of the kingdom of God manifest themselves counterculturally. López continues, 'The kingdom of God does not define itself by status or by one individual's ability to rule over another, but it does so by the ability to serve others in a sacrificial way and by our willingness to give our life for the love of our neighbor'.[103] In other words, the church has not been called to be lord over others but to be the servant of all.

---

[99] This is a point on which both Villafañe and López agree. Cf. López, *Pentecostalismo y misión integral*; López and Waldrop, 'The God of Life and the Spirit of Life'.

[100] López and Waldrop, 'The God of Life and the Spirit of Life', p. 3.

[101] Speaking of how Christ's followers should live in the world, López states, 'He expects his disciples to be a countercultural society when measured against civil society, an alternative community radically different from other human societies'. López, *La propuesta política del Reino de Dios*, p. 33. All translations from this work are my translation.

[102] López, *La propuesta política del reino de Dios*, p. 41.

[103] López, *La propuesta política del Reino de Dios*, p. 35.

Before moving on to López's public contributions, let me mention one last ecclesial contribution. In *Pentecostalismo y misión integral*, López underscores the need to be an *iglesia integral* (a wholistic church). This concept of *iglesia integral* builds on the Latin American theme of *misión integral*.[104] In the book's preface, René Padilla testifies to this by affirming that *una iglesia integral* is 'one that refuses to separate that which is religious from that which is public and faith from works'.[105] Moreover, states Padilla, *una iglesia integral* must be driven by *una espiritualidad integral* (wholistic spirituality). This spiritual wholeness is not only concerned with the inner life of the church, but also 'it calls for a missionary agenda that has on its horizon the church's involvement in public spaces as part of civil society'.[106] Thus, López challenges the Pentecostal church to expand her traditional understanding of missional spaces and to include spaces that might seem 'nontraditional' but are nonetheless in need of reconciliation, justice, and the impact of the liberating Spirit of God.

---

[104] The foundation for *misión integral* came from the *Fraternidad Teológica Latinoamericana* (FTL, Latin American Theological Fellowship) in the 1970s. René Padilla, who was part of the early leadership of the FTL, wrote: 'It was the result of becoming aware of the need to return to the biblical text in search of elements that would help God's people fulfill their role in history in light of their covenant with Christ and in response to their context'. Hence, *misión integral* is the attempt to understand how Christ's salvific event responds not only to the spiritual need of the people but also to their present physical needs. Furthermore, 'The movement of *misión integral* emerged as a roadway of reflection and practice committed to God and to the world, seeking to create new spaces of faith where current and future generations could move to promote the kingdom of God'. See Harold Segura, 'La misión integral: Treinta y cinco años después', *Espacio de Diálogo* 2 (April 2005). My translation.

[105] René Padilla, 'Preface', in López, *Pentecostalismo y misión integral*, p. 7. All translation from this work are my translation.

[106] Even so, López sees the Pentecostal community as countercultural. She is one among many components in society. This line of thought resonates with Benjamin Valentin's proposal of public theology. Valentin proposes that liberation theologies need to see themselves as counter-public voices that are within a greater public realm. 'Latino/a theologians can enhance the theoretical scope of their theology and might also heighten its sociopolitical relevance in the national context, by directly engaging the question of what tasks and features characterize public discourse and, correspondingly, the role of "public intellectual"'. Thus, he explains, as we see ourselves within our own struggles and also see the commonalities that exist between movements, we can achieve a greater good and a greater justice. See René Padilla, 'Preface', p. 11; Benjamin Valentin, *Mapping Public Theology: Beyond Culture, Identity, and Difference* (Harrisburg, PA: Trinity Press, 2002).

Contributions for a Lived Ecclesiology

A common thread between Luvis, Villafañe, and López is the public nature of the Pentecostal community. Yet I understand López's work to be nearly the poster child of such integration. In fact, he sounds a clarion call with, 'It should be clear that for a Spirit-filled disciple, there is no dichotomy between the spiritual and the material; the religious and the secular; the private and the public; because God's purpose points toward the reconciliation of all'.[107] What follows is a summary of his proposal for a lived ecclesiology.

In López's thought, there is a clear connection between the Person of the Holy Spirit and the church's public calling. López cannot fathom an individual/community filled with Spirit who has no sense of engaging the public. His reading of Acts 2 sustains this connectivity. In the end, he concludes that there is a seamless relationship between the baptism of the Holy Spirit and *misión integral* (integral mission); and such relationships become manifest through the construction of public testimony.[108]

In addition, in the previous section I mentioned that one of the themes that López has developed is the church's ethical dimension, which is founded on God's kingdom ethics. This ethical commitment is not only dependent on spiritual preparation, which López recognizes as important, but moreover, it is important to have a solid and concrete understanding of the public arena. In other words, López poignantly states that the church needs to be knowledgeable of what is happening in the public arena and become aware of how to navigate the complexities of such an arena.[109] According to López, the landscape of Latin America has changed drastically. This change has affected the attitude and way of life of the church. Thus, the church – directly or indirectly – has surfaced as a new actor and voice seeking to engage culture by way of social and political realms through her religious beliefs. López understands that the move toward such engagement was inevitable. 'The evangelical communities are inserted in society; thus, they cannot be oblivious to the concrete public

---

[107] López, *Pentecostalismo y misión integral*, p. 12.

[108] For a thorough commentary on Acts 2, see López, *Pentecostalismo y misión integral*, pp. 17–53.

[109] López and Arroyo, *Tejiendo un nuevo rostro público*, Kindle, 250.Introduction, section 1. All translations from this work are my translation.

scenario.'[110] Therefore, the church's border crossing into the public arena should be understood as an ethical commitment.

This integral/wholistic understanding of the church's mission, in turn, raises the question of discourses. On the one hand, the church in the world speaks the language of the gospel. On the other hand, López underscores that this language must engage and speak to the contextual realities. Thus, the church 'has to articulate a public discourse that is consistent and relevant to our reality, forged organically from the community of faith, to defend the dignity of all human beings; a discourse that is supported by a consistent commitment to the collective struggle for social justice, peace, and reconciliation'.[111] This discourse is not fanatic nor is it a fundamentalist sermon, both of which overshadow the dialoguing partner (the public arena) or the benefactor of our discourse (all human beings). On the contrary, it is a prophetic pronouncement that has both the public realm and humanity at its epicenter. Yet, for López, Pentecostals have much work left in this area. Therefore, the development of such discourse must be at the top of the Pentecostal to-do-list.[112]

A final point that I want to express is that any God-led activity is in and of itself a political pronouncement. For López, all divine actions manifested in this world come as a critical stance against humanly motivated actions. And if the church is truly the spokesman of the gospel, this is a responsibility that she cannot renounce. Using the prophet Amos as an example, López states that the prophet accepted such an 'uncomfortable calling'[113] because it was a 'nonnegotiable task'.[114] According to López, that was both his task and nature as a prophet of God:

> His presence and interventions in the public life of his community made him visible and expressed his ability to uncover the

---

[110] López and Arroyo, *Tejiendo un nuevo rostro público*, Kindle loc. 244, Introduction, section 1.

[111] López and Arroyo, *Tejiendo un nuevo rostro público*, Kindle loc. 1306, Chapter 3, section 1.

[112] Along with the development of a public discourse, López mentions four other areas of need. (1) The recognition and empowerment of Christians who can serve in the public arena. (2) The involvement of Christians within political parties and social movements. (3) The development of models of responsible citizenship. (4) The expansion of the horizon of political and social relations. See López and Arroyo, *Tejiendo un nuevo rostro público*, Kindle loc. 1477–2705, chapter 5.

[113] López, *La propuesta política del Reino de Dios*, p. 46.

[114] López, *La propuesta política del Reino de Dios*, p. 47.

contemporary idols and to challenge and publicly denounce temporal authorities when they move away from such practices as justice and the defense of the human rights of those who are defenseless.[115]

In other words, López accentuates that, for Amos, there was no question about his public responsibility. Amos knew what was happening in the midst of his society, and he could not avoid it.[116]

Conclusion

This chapter has analyzed the theological contributions of three Latino/a Pentecostal scholars who are wholeheartedly concerned with the nature, life, and mission of the church and its engagement in the public sphere. Based on their areas of expertise, special attention was given to the church and equality; the church and social justice; and the church and the polis. What can be gained from this analysis?

First, all three scholars agree that the public character of the Pentecostal church is infused with the Spirit's agency. Just as the Spirit moves everywhere and in everything, there are no boundaries in terms of space; thus, the Pentecostal church must bring down the wall between the sacred and the public and make her presence known. Yet this point encounters some challenges. According to Luvis, 'The strong emphasis on the spiritual life [of Pentecostals] has produced a silence in the church toward an integral approach to the whole creation'.[117] Such silence, according to these theologians, is a misunderstanding of what it is to walk and live in the Spirit.

Second, their understanding of the church's role in society is seriously informed by context. For example, the descriptors 'egalitarian church', 'servant church', and 'integral church' are images that are

---

[115] López, *La propuesta política del Reino de Dios*, p. 46.

[116] López's understanding of the church as a prophetic voice is congruent with the role that Brueggemann describes of the prophet.

Here it is argued that they were concerned with most elemental changes in human society and that they understood a great deal about how change is effected … They understood the strange incongruence between public conviction and personal yearning. Most of all, they understood the distinctive power of language, the capacity to speak in ways that evoke newness 'fresh from the word'.

For an in-depth study of the role of the prophet, see Walter Brueggemann, *The Prophetic Imagination* (Minneapolis, MN: Fortress Press, 2nd edn, 2001), p. xxiii.

[117] Luvis, 'Sewing a New Cloth', pp. 175–76.

informed by their contextual realities. In the words of Sigurd Berg-man, it seems that there is a continual conversation between religion and the city;[118] and this conversation has serious implications for our theologies. And these are mutually informed.

Third, though Luvis, Villafañe, and López develop unique theo-logical contributions, there is a common understanding: the ecclesi-ologies they are constructing are representative of God's kingdom in this world. Consequently, these communities manifest themselves as re-imagined communities that seek to intervene in concrete socio-political contexts and establish themselves not as escape routes but as redeeming communities.

Fourth, each theologian agrees that the church's *diakonia* is key in the development of a public character that sets the foundation for a lived ecclesiology. She is not called to self-indulge but to know the times and be able to serve and respond to the needs of the Other wholistically.

To what extent are these contributions congruent with what is ac-tively occurring in the Pentecostal church? The following chapter will describe the results of an ethnographic study that was done in a Pen-tecostal church in Puerto Rico. Attention will be given to the way liturgy informs how Pentecostals engage public spaces and how the public sphere informs their liturgy.

---

[118] Sigurd Bergman, 'Lived Religion in Lived Spaces', in Heinz Streib, Astrid Dinter, and Kerstin Söderblom (eds.), *Lived Religion: Conceptual, Empirical and Practi-cal-Theological Approaches: Essays in Honor of Hans-Günter Heimbrock* (Boston: Brill, 2008), p. 200.

4

LIVING WATERS: A CASE STUDY OF *RÍOS DE AGUA VIVA* CHURCH

Belief and Life

As stated in Chapter 1, this study is founded on two approaches. The first seeks to understand how Pentecostal theologians have theologized about what it means to be the church and about the church's responsibility in public spaces. The second focuses on how *el culto* (the worship service) forms its members to live their faith in their lived spaces. In the previous chapter, I attempted to answer the first by analyzing the contributions of three Latina/o Pentecostal theologians, Agustina Luvis Núñez, Eldin Villafañe, and Darío López. All three manifest an intimate and natural relationship between beliefs and life experiences. Furthermore, they also agree that it is in *el culto* where this relationship is nurtured and where the public character of Pentecostals is constructed. Hence, if *el culto* is the space in which the public character of Pentecostals is formed, how does this happen?

This chapter will attempt to answer this question using an ethnographic approach. In the words of Peter Ward, 'To understand the church, we should view it as being simultaneously theological and social/cultural'.[1] Thus, it is important to understand what happens when the church gathers as a community of believers. In addition, Mark Cartledge affirms that Pentecostals need to 'interject into the abstract systematic and historically oriented discourse' the insight and

---

[1] Peter Ward, *Perspectives on Ecclesiology and Ethnography* (Studies in Ecclesiology and Ethnography; Grand Rapids, MI: Eerdmans, 2012), p. 2.

value 'from concrete empirical studies'.[2] Such an interdisciplinary approach, he adds, will better serve the future of Pentecostal studies.

Welcome to RAV[3]

The *Iglesia de Dios Mission Board* (IDDMB) *'Ríos de Agua Viva'* (RAV) has been present in the town of Aguas Buenas for forty-two years. Aguas Buenas is a small mountainous town with a population of 28,659.[4] It is located almost forty kilometers from San Juan, toward the east-central area of the island of Puerto Rico and known for the fresh water springs that run through the area, which gave the town its name, Aguas Buenas.[5]

The drive up to Aguas Buenas is a beautiful one. Once you leave the expressway and take Road 156 towards the mountain, it is a straight drive of twenty minutes to the heart of the town (though I must confess that my first visit seventeen years ago was not so straight or that quick due to the off-road conditions of the previous route). There is not much movement when you get into the town on Sundays. As you arrive at the only intersection with a traffic light, you can either keep going straight or turn left. Most of those who keep going straight are congregants that are either going to the Catholic Church or the Baptist Church which are on the town square. However, those who make a left are driving towards RAV.

Suddenly, you see a plateau with two buildings, one of them identified with a big cross and signage that reads *Iglesia Ríos de Agua Viva* with a logo of a mountain divided with a stream of water. The other building is a remodeled two-story house that has a cafeteria and classrooms on the first floor and a youth church on the second. As you begin to drive into their seven-acre lot you are received by the parking attendants who state, *'Dios te bendiga, bienvenido a RAV'* ('God bless you, welcome to RAV'), followed by instructions on where and how to park. As you walk up the hill towards the sanctuary you can hear the people greeting each other, servers instructing others where to park and children running outside regardless of being dressed up for Sunday service – in 90 degrees and 85 percent of humidity.

---

[2] Cartledge, 'Renewal Ecclesiology in Empirical Perspective', p. 64.

[3] Apart from pastors Willy and Miriam, the rest of the names used in this ethnography are fictional. This is to maintain the anonymity of the informants.

[4] This is according to the 2010 census. See 'Censo 2010 Puerto Rico' (Departamento de Comercio de EE.UU., 2012), 1–3, www.census.gov.

[5] A possible translation could be, 'Good Waters'.

Once in the sanctuary, you are received by ushers who not only stretch their hands to you in greeting with a big smile on their faces, but also pull you into their chest and hug you as they welcome you, '*Dios te bendiga, esta es tu casa*' ('God bless you, this is your home'). As they direct you to your cushioned chair, they inquire about you and your family. This conversation gives them the opportunity to know if you are regular congregant or a visitor. If the latter, they give you a welcome packet and pass your name to the person that will recognize the visitors during the service.

The sanctuary has both a traditional and contemporary feeling. For example, upholding the traditional aspect, as you look to the altar you can see the cross, the communion table, the pulpit, and the chairs where the pastors sit. Yet, in contrast, there are projection screens, instruments of a full worship band (electric guitars and bass, keyboards, and full drums-set), lighting set, smoke machine, and a sound system that caters to the musicians and at least six vocal microphones. Moreover, this traditional-contemporary theme is heightened as congregants begin to walk the aisles of the sanctuary. There is a mix of jeans and khakis; dresses and T-shirts; suits and slim jackets; high heels and TOMS (casual shoes). Nevertheless, as the service begins, whatever differences exist are overtaken by their coming together as one worshiping community.

Ten minutes before the start of the service, a team member comes to the pulpit and invites everyone to greet one another. Immediately, you begin to hear a low murmur which then turns into a loud fellowship moment. Then as people begin to retake their places (after a few calls of order from the stage) the team member begins to read scripture. Once the reading has ended, the person shares some words or testimony about what was read and then leads the church in a communal prayer. As the prayer moves along and intensifies, the musicians approach their instruments, and they begin to play and establish the rhythm of the first song. Feeding from the intensity of the prayer and from the chords played by the musicians, some congregants begin to shout, others raise their voice as they pray, an old lady begins to praise with her *maracas* (shakers), the pastor begins to jump as he plays his *pandereta* (tambourine), and others raise their hand as if they are surrendering. As the prayer comes to an end, the church replies with a loud, *¡AMÉN!*, as a way of affirming the prayer and at the same time signaling their readiness to begin *el culto* (worship service).

Those who had been part of the church prior to the arrival of pastors Willy and Miriam affirm that there is a difference between what was known as the *Iglesia* of Barriada Vázquez (Vázquez Hood) – the old name of the church – and what is known today as *Iglesia* RAV. Willy and Miriam changed the church's name to underscore their sense of community and to give a clear mission of who they wanted it to be. As a result, for the past sixteen years RAV has become 'a stream of living waters' in Aguas Buenas and even beyond this town.

A Snapshot of RAV

RAV is a community on the move. Whether you visit during Wednesday, Friday, or Sunday services, it does not take long to see how active this church is. Activities are going on throughout the whole campus, and visitors get a sense of that; as the name states, the congregation is a *living stream of water.*

According to pastor Willy, the church has over thirty ministries, and they are on full display usually in Sunday morning service. 'Not only do we have ministries that serve certain age groups, but we have also developed ministries that focus on particular needs, whether within the church or the community.'[6] Carmen, a woman who recently began attending the church, confirmed this when she inquired about serving in RAV: 'I don't know – there are so many things to do. I need to sort them out and find where I'm going to serve.'[7]

RAV is a diverse community. A glimpse at those in attendance testifies to this fact. The diversity is manifested in many ways. For example, RAV has a wide age representation. Though the median age of those attending is in the forties, they have ministries serving newborns all the way to senior adults. Furthermore, RAV has created a space in which farmers, teachers, accountants, pharmacists, the unemployed, recovering addicts, and stay-at-home parents can sit together to worship as a community. As one of their mottos says, 'Our doors are wide open'.[8] Everyone is welcome.

RAV is an informed community. This informed character is dual in nature. On the one hand, RAV is a community that places a high value on education, whether formal or informal. One of the

---

[6] Pastor Willy. 2016. Interviewed by author. Aguas Buenas, PR. May 25.

[7] Carmen. 2016. Interviewed by author. Aguas Buenas, PR. June 3.

[8] Pastor Willy. 2016. Interviewed by author. Aguas Buenas, PR. May 25.

important programs that RAV has developed in the last five years is what they have called 'the RAV training route'.[9]

This educational program has various levels, but those who want to serve in any capacity in the church must complete the whole program. On the other hand, RAV is a church that is well informed about issues related to the surrounding communities. Whether in *el culto* (worship service) or during informal conversations, you can hear congregants referring to pressing issues related to politics and economics among other.[10]

Finally, the members of the RAV community are proud of their Pentecostal heritage. Puerto Rican Christianity has been greatly impacted by Pentecostalism. Pentecostalism arrived in Puerto Rico on the heels of the Protestant missionary endeavor. Thus, there is a high sense of the agency of the Holy Spirit in Puerto Rican religiosity. Yet RAV has emphasized the Holy Spirit not only as an identity marker, but even more, members have made intentional strides to let this understanding shape their life as a community of faith and as citizens.

Beyond the Temple

For Serene Jones and The Workgroup on Constructive Christian Theology, 'our religious beliefs can almost never be separated from other beliefs, actions, and attitudes that we hold and that also shape us, such as our culturally constructed beliefs about what it means to be a woman or a citizen or a student of theology'.[11] Thus, our religious experiences are manifested in all areas of life. All three Pentecostal theologians analyzed in Chapter 3 agree in saying that *el culto* (worship service) is the place where the public character of the believer is formed. This formation occurs in the midst of communal participation through prayers, *coritos* (songs), testimonies, Scripture, and preaching, among other elements.[12] Hence, if *el culto* is the place

---

[9] Pastor Miriam. 2016. Interviewed by author. Aguas Buenas, PR. May 5.

[10] These two topics were the most pressing due to the coinciding of my visit with the general elections' campaigning season.

[11] The Workgroup on Constructive Christian Theology, *Constructive Theology: A Contemporary Approach to Classic Themes: A Project of The Workgroup on Constructive Christian Theology* (Minneapolis: Augsburg Fortress Publishers, 2005), p. 11.

[12] For a description of a Latino Pentecostal service, see Wilmer Estrada-Carrasquillo, 'Taking the Risk: The Openness and Attentiveness of Latin American Pentecostal Worship', in Lee Roy Martin (ed.), *Toward a Pentecostal Theology of Worship* (Cleveland, TN: CPT Press, 2015), pp. 235–46.

where the public character of Pentecostals is constructed, how does this happen?

Participant Observation: A Narrative

My association with RAV began approximately seventeen years ago. I first learned about this church through pastor Willy and pastor Miriam. Before their arrival to RAV, Willy and Miriam served as assistant pastors at my local church. Hence, after the appointment to RAV, those who were close to them shared their transitional process. Since then, I have visited RAV sporadically, whether to preach, sing, or just to participate as a guest during special events. Thus, in some way or another, I have seen from afar the development that this community of faith has experienced from *Barriada Vazquez* church to RAV church.

Despite my close relationship with pastor Willy and pastor Miriam, I probably visited them only once or twice per year. These long breaks between visits allowed me to perceive the transformation of this church vividly. In retrospect, three things stood out. One was their shift from an exclusive or closed mindset community to an inclusive and open-door community. The demographics of the church changed drastically from a homogenous community to a more heterogeneous one (e.g. educational level, class, occupation, and age). Another was their impact within the surrounding communities of the church. Looking back to their journey, I can say that pastor Willy and pastor Miriam were instrumental in teaching RAV to become a missional church. Notwithstanding the other churches that were in the vicinity, based on the ethnographic date I could see that the community recognized RAV as a church that constantly engaged them. Lastly, which is a product of the other two, was the exponential growth in attendance. When I first visited them, there were no more than 30 people in attendance. In early 2011, just when I was moving to the United States, 450 people were attending any given Sunday.

As I thought about the implementation of my ethnographic study, RAV was one among the few churches that fit the criteria that I was looking for. I was interested in understanding how beliefs inform the way people engage the public and RAV turned out to be the viable option; RAV had become a church that embodied such an integrative spirituality. In addition, I was close enough – relationally and theologically – that I would have access to internal and valid information that would help me in the ethnography. Finally, due to my move to the US in 2011, I was physically detached enough and educationally trained to the extent that I would be able to see them in a fresh way.

Integrative Nature/Character of RAV's Liturgy

As I arrived at RAV, I was interested in observing the ways in which the congregation's liturgy (prayers, songs, Scripture readings, sermons, etc.) *directly* engaged public issues or themes. Moreover, in what ways are public issues influencing their liturgy (prayers, songs, Scripture readings, sermons, etc.), and how frequently – directly or indirectly – do these themes occur? Finally, how do their beliefs inform their public actions?

During my fieldwork, I was able to observe that RAV's meetings – Wednesday prayer, Friday Bible school, and Sunday worship service – are full of integrative language. In other words, there is a conversation between the lived faith and the lived spaces. Below I narrate my observations.

Biblical education is central to RAV's liturgy. As mentioned above, all members who seek to serve in any capacity in the church need to join the RAV training program, which is offered as needed. However, RAV also meets every Friday as a 'community to study the Bible, to exegete it, and to apply it to our everyday experiences'.[13] Prior to my arrival they had started a series focused on the book of James.

During my first visit they were studying Jas 5.7–15. After reading these verses, the group focused on the theme of judging others. Immediately, pastor Miriam said, 'Let me make clear that judgment is restorative, as long as it is done right'.[14] Then she recalled the case of a judge in Aguadilla, PR. She explained,

> Regardless of his responsibility to represent rightly both law and justice, this man is not immune to corrupt behavior. Therefore, knowing and having the instruments to act or judge rightly does not guarantee that we will do it. Unfortunately, this man went to jail. Similarly, as the body of Christ, we are not exempt from behaving wrongly, unless we seek God continually.[15]

---

[13] Pastor Miriam. 2016. Field notes by author, Aguas Buenas, PR. May 27.
[14] Pastor Miriam. 2016. Field notes by author, Aguas Buenas, PR. May 27.
[15] Pastor Miriam. 2016. Field notes by author, Aguas Buenas, PR. May 27.

For pastor Miriam, it was important to convey the message of the social responsibility of Christians. It is not that we know *what* to do, but that we act in the right *way*. As she stated, 'This is practiced in everyday situations'.[16]

RAV prayer meetings also had the same integrative flavor. Pastor Willy was clear about the purpose of their prayer meetings: 'RAV prayer nights are not only done with those we see around us, but RAV is also part of a larger church body that prays and continues to pray'.[17] I found this rather interesting because, though committed to its community and local ministry, RAV is very aware that she is part of a universal body. For Charles Van Engen, this is an example of an in-tune church. Van Engen states, a 'truly catholic local group of believers is in fact the local manifestation of the universal glocal church'.[18] Moreover, pastor Willy adds that their prayer is not a mere metaphysical event or dislocated from the realities of this world, but, on the contrary, 'When we pray we stand in the gap for others, and we are living in a moment where our nation needs us to stand in that gap'.[19]

The prayer meetings observed were full of allusions to issues of public matter. For example, during prayer service that was led by the men's ministry,[20] the theme was geared around the processes of constructing a building. They presented a skit in which a man was trying to build up his character to Jesus' image. The skit was interrupted by prayers led by someone representing the men's ministry, and each one helped the man in the skit grow closer to Jesus' image. Regarding this, the leader of the men said, 'When we are in the process of constructing something, there are steps that need to be taken to complete the task. Similarly, as Christians, we are in a process of building who we are up into the image of Jesus.'[21] He also added that 'the Holy Spirit is the only agent capable of transforming the human condition and the crisis that Puerto Rico is going through'.[22] Immediately, he asked

---

16 Pastor Miriam. 2016. Field notes by author, Aguas Buenas, PR. May 27.

17 Pastor Willy. 2016. Fieldnotes by author. Aguas Buenas, PR. June 1.

18 Charles E. Van Engen, 'The Glocal Church: Locality and Catholicity in a Globalizing World', in Craig Ott and Harold A. Netland (eds.), *Globalizing Theology: Belief and Practice in an Era of World Christianity* (Grand Rapids, MI: Baker Academic, 2006), p. 179.

19 Pastor Willy. 2016. Field notes by author. Aguas Buenas, PR. June 1.

20 All ministries rotate leading Wednesday prayer meeting.

21 Men's leader. 2016. Field notes by author. Aguas Buenas, PR June 1.

22 Men's leader. 2016. Field notes by author. Aguas Buenas, PR June 1.

the whole church to pray for 'God's intervention in these difficult times to make each and every one of them a living testimony to those who are losing their faith and facing economic problems'.[23]

The other night of prayer was organized around the theme of joy, and there were four prayer sessions. Each one focused on a specific aspect of the theme: surpassing joy, restorative joy, longstanding joy, and justice, peace, and joy. For the leader of the consolidation ministry,[24] these characteristics of joy are vividly experienced within the Acts 2.47 community. This New Testament church community plays a major role in Pentecostal ecclesiology. First, it is established after the coming of the Holy Spirit over those in the Upper Room. Second, as a result, many Pentecostals sees this community as a model.[25] Concerning this, she added, 'and as Pentecostals this is something that we need to emulate'.[26] Furthermore, a common thread through the prayer sessions was that Puerto Rico needed these different forms of joy to be manifested. For example, the person leading the prayer of restorative joy highlighted the need for 'God to restore the present governmental and societal crisis in the nation'.[27]

As we can see through these examples, RAV prayer sessions are interconnected to their contextual issues. Interestingly, it was hard to decipher what was informing what. Were their themes connecting to these public issues, or were the issues informing the prayers?

Of the three weekly meetings, Sunday may be the service in which one can experience in fullest display the interconnectivity of the public sphere with RAV's liturgy. Whether through songs, scriptures, testimonies, prayers, exhortations, or preaching, the constant dialogue between their lived faith and their lived spaces is evident.

One of my visits coincided with Pentecost Sunday. The atmosphere in the sanctuary was charged with a sense of expectancy. In conversations prior to the start of the service, I heard people saying they were ready to receive 'a special visit from the Holy Spirit'.[28] The

---

[23] Men's leader. 2016. Field notes by author. Aguas Buenas, PR June 1.

[24] This ministry is focused in connecting the new converts and visitors to the different ministries in the church.

[25] For an example of how Pentecostals have read and appropriated this New Testament community see, Gastón Espinosa, *Latino Pentecostals in America: Faith and Politics in Action* (Cambridge, MA: Harvard University Press, 2014), p. 187.

[26] Consolidation leader. 2016. Field notes by author. Aguas Buenas, PR. June 8.

[27] Participant. 2016. Field notes by author. Aguas Buenas, PR. June 8.

[28] Observations. 2016. Field notes by author. Aguas Buenas, PR. May 29.

service started with the opening words of pastor Willy. He began by affirming that 'Today's celebration is not only a remembrance or a looking back to a historical event, but today also serves as a reaffirmation of the agency and work of the Holy Spirit, here and now'.[29] He then added, 'He [the Holy Spirit] has and still is moving today … There is still Holy Spirit for today'.[30] Following these words, he reminded the church that there are some who question the movement and agency of the Holy Spirit. Yet, he emphatically voiced, 'The manifestation of the Holy Spirit has not finished; baptism with the Holy Spirit has not ceased'.[31]

Following these opening words, the worship team led the church in songs that invited the Holy Spirit into their midst (*Ven, Espíritu, ven; Come Holy Spirit, Come*); affirmed God's presence among them (*El Señor está en este lugar; The Lord is here*); and recognized the incoming of the Spirit (*Algo está cayendo aquí; Something is falling here*) and the anointing of the Spirit over the church (*Hay una unción aquí; There is an anointing here*).[32] Pastor Miriam spoke in between songs about the theology and praxis of the Pentecostal church. For example, she stated, 'The Pentecostal church is a voice for the community'.[33] She followed this statement by explaining, 'This voice is not only for those inside [the church] but also for those outside [in society]'. What she was trying to convey was that not only does RAV speak for the church and into the world, but also the church has a responsibility to listen to the world and speak for it. She grounded her statements in Scripture, saying that this is what we read in Acts 1.8, where 'the church has been called to be a witness through the infilling of the Holy Spirit'.[34]

Neither pastor Miriam nor pastor Willy preached that particular morning. They invited Elizabeth Resto, who is the first woman to be elected as a presiding bishop of any Pentecostal denomination in Puerto Rico.[35] Though at first I was discouraged, I expected Willy or Miriam to preach that day, in the end it was helpful to understand

---

[29] Pastor Willy. 2016. Field notes by author. Aguas Buenas, PR. May 29.

[30] Pastor Willy. 2016. Field notes by author. Aguas Buenas, PR. May 29.

[31] Pastor Willy. 2016. Field notes by author. Aguas Buenas, PR. May 29.

[32] Observations. 2016. Field notes by author. Aguas Buenas, PR. May 29.

[33] Pastor Miriam. 2016. Field notes by author. Aguas Buenas, PR. May 29.

[34] Pastor Miriam. 2016. Field notes by author. Aguas Buenas, PR. May 29.

[35] She leads the *Iglesia Cristo Misionera*, an indigenous Pentecostal church established in 1935.

that there is a sense of public orientation within Pentecostal preaching. Two things stood out in Resto's sermon. First, she shared a testimony of divine healing that occurred during a mission trip. In this particular event, God's divine touch not only healed the sick body of the person affected but also brought transformation to the community where this person lived. Resto then affirmed this testimony by emphatically saying, 'Divine healing is both a personal and a social transformative experience'.[36] Furthermore, Resto underscored the continuity between *el culto* and what happens afterwards. By continuity she meant, 'The Holy Spirit is not only given for *el culto* (worship service), it is also given in order to operate when we go back home'.[37] In other words, the manifestation and infilling of the Holy Spirit is both a living faith experience and a living life experience. This understanding of the Spirit with us as we go is central to RAV – so much so that in the benediction, pastor Willy commissioned the church with the following words, 'Pentecost [i.e. lived faith] is more than what has happened in the service today, Pentecost goes with us as we walk away from the church and we immerse ourselves in our schools, work, community, and everywhere we go [lived spaces]'.[38]

The next Sunday that I had the opportunity to visit, they were celebrating mission Sunday. RAV is a missionary church.[39] Regarding this, the missions leader said, 'We are a missionary church, and we need to move away from our comfort zone'.[40] Using Abraham's story, she added, 'God is calling all of his sons and daughters, because our nation needs all of us. Therefore, we need to move out from our comfort zones.'[41] Immediately, she referenced different cultural challenges as a way of inviting the church to move from that comfortable state. 'Just as it happened with Abraham and Jesus, let us step beyond our areas of comfort.'[42]

---

[36] Elizabeth Resto. 2016. Field notes by author. Aguas Buenas, PR. May 29.

[37] Elizabeth Resto. 2016. Field notes by author. Aguas Buenas, PR. May 29.

[38] Pastor Willy. 2016. Field notes by author. Aguas Buenas, PR. May 20.

[39] RAV sustains or has connections to projects or missionaries in Ecuador, Panama, Paraguay, Argentina, Honduras, and China. Every other month, they celebrate mission Sunday to update the church on the different projects and to raise financial help.

[40] Missions leader. 2016. Field notes by author. Augas Buenas, PR. June 26.

[41] Missions leader. 2016. Field notes by author. Augas Buenas, PR. June 26.

[42] Missions leader. 2016. Field notes by author. Augas Buenas, PR. June 26.

In her final statement, the leader of the mission's ministry affirmed the indigenous (local) and pilgrim (universal) nature of RAV. She stated, 'This church transcends far beyond our contours, and we can see what God is doing through us'.[43] This immanent and transcendent character of RAV was vividly experienced during this service. On the one hand, this service highlighted some of the work that RAV was doing in Paraguay, and the sermon was preached by a member of RAV who was a missionary to Argentina. On the other hand, the worship leader made the church aware of difficulties the nation was facing. It was very clear from the beginning that the political and economic state of Puerto Rico was on her mind. The songs spoke about opening the heavens (*Abre los cielos*); about the church crying out for God to descend with power (*Tu iglesia clama hoy*); and about being rescued from present trials (*Canción de redención*). Moreover, I found it interesting that the worship leader interconnected the present state of the nation with the state of *el culto*, saying that one is dependent on the other. She added,

> In the times of Ezekiel, *el culto* became contaminated, and this brought a national crisis. Yet in times of crisis like these, God raises up leadership and people that can be of testimony to the world. For example, Daniel was able to step out and serve in a government position and become an agent of transformation and a conduit of hope and peace.[44]

Such words have profound implications for the church's public character. Moreover, this statement brings a perspective that is not common. Usually, the common sentiment is that the church has become a reflection of what is happening in culture. However, the worship leader's reading of Ezekiel and Daniel gave her a different understanding, that is, the state of the church has much to say about the state of state of the polis.

The sermon kept pressing this point of view. The missionary/preacher talked about what it meant to be light amid chaos. She began by stating that the church, 'rather than being surprised by what is happening in the world, needs to grieve and to take action'.[45]

---

[43] Missions leader. 2016. Field notes by author. Augas Buenas, PR. June 26.

[44] Worship leader. 2016. Field notes by author. Aguas Buenas, PR. June 26.

[45] RAV Missionary to Argentina. 2016. Field notes by author, Aguas Buenas, PR. June 26.

According to her, the church needs to stop complaining and, instead, needs to lament and move. Furthermore, she stated that to be light in a world in chaos, 'We must rediscover what it means to be sensitive to the Other'.[46] It seemed to her that the church is becoming more hostile than hospitable. Furthermore, she raised a very important point about the nature and character of the church:

> If we proclaim to the world what is to be done, but the world finds no righteousness in us, there is no value in our words. We cannot ask the government for justice, peace, and truth and meanwhile we live in contradiction to what we are asking for. There is an intrinsic connection between our faith and life. Our preaching and faith demand from us a congruent lifestyle. We cannot ask of others that which we are not able to do as a church and as citizens.[47]

One of my last Sundays was a very emotional meeting for RAV. The Wednesday prior to that meeting, one of the youth leaders, who was twenty-six years old, died suddenly from a heart attack. That Sunday, pastor Willy, rather that preaching, reflected on the difficult experience of death. Prior to sharing his closing thoughts, he referenced Paul's words to those at Colossae: 'Whatever you do in word or deed, do all in the name of the Lord Jesus, giving thanks through Him to God the Father' (Col. 3.17). Consequently, he immediately praised the youth leader as someone who really understood what it meant to be not of this world but to live for it. As he spoke about the life of this young man, he said,

> You probably never saw him standing at this altar preaching a sermon, you probably never saw him holding the microphone to lead worship or something similar, but he was very clear about his faith, his Pentecostal experience, and how to live a life guided by those experiences ... And you know why I can say all this with such certainty, because this church has never gathered more than five hundred people in attendance, but last Friday, as we celebrated the life of this young man, over eight hundred came to this sanctuary, because of the life that this young man modeled to them. He

---

[46] RAV Missionary to Argentina. 2016. Field notes by author, Aguas Buenas, PR. June 26.
[47] RAV Missionary to Argentina. 2016. Field notes by author, Aguas Buenas, PR. June 26.

traded the microphone for a whistle; the tie for an umpire mask; the suit for a referee uniform; and the parish ministry for a prison ministry. He lived his faith; he was a true living epistle.[48]

As stated at the beginning of this section, RAV's liturgy is rich with public symbols, characteristics, and references. But for them, this is something somewhat implicit. My last night with them, I was asked to share some words about the study. In a very simple way, I tried to summarize the many ways that their liturgy was interconnected with public issues and events. After I finished, they were amazed at the integrative nature of their liturgy. Such integration affirms not only how liturgy informs their public character but also how the public sphere is at play as they worship as a community.

Focus Group: A Narrative

As a manner of unpacking the findings from my observation, I met every two weeks with a representative group of the church membership.[49] Our conversations focused on three areas: background questions, church and society questions, and theological/liturgical questions.[50]

Background

These questions played an important role in setting the context. First, they helped establish a connection between all the participants. Second, these questions served as an entry point into the life story of the participants. Third, they were foundational for setting the broader context of the conversation. More than a retelling of their story, for Pentecostals, this becomes a testimonial event, in which one can learn about the character of the church and the individual and how the divine presence of God has been at work in them.

There were three main questions within this section. The first asked how they came to be a part of RAV. The second asked about their longevity in the church. The final question inquired about how their understanding of what it means to 'be' church has been redefined since coming to RAV.

---

[48] Pastor Willy. 2016. Field notes by author. Aguas Buenas, PR. July 3.

[49] See appendix A for a description of the adopted sampling and selecting process. The focus group was comprised of ten people. The names, as stated in chapter 1, are fictitious.

[50] See the Ethnographic Question Guide in appendix B.

The ways the focus group members came to RAV and their reasons for staying, in one way or another, speak about the missional character of RAV. Antonio came to RAV while he was going through a difficult crisis. During that time, he was a member at another church, but he decided that moving to a new community would be better for him. According to Antonio, 'As soon as I came in, I did not feel like a stranger'.[51] Thanks to that hospitality, Antonio has been part of RAV for six years.

Carmen, one of the newest members in the church at the time of my visit, came to know about RAV by way of a missionary trip that was planned to her native country. According to Carmen, she was amazed by the compassion and the work that RAV displayed during the visit. This experience awakened her desire to visit RAV. After that first visit, Carmen moved to Puerto Rico and has become a member.

Pedro, the elder of the group, has been at RAV for almost twelve years. He came to the church through an invitation from his daughter. Pedro mentions, 'It isn't that I wasn't a Christian, I just used to go to another church',[52] but he decided to respond to his daughter's invitation. 'I found something here that I didn't have in the previous church, which was the Holy Spirit, and I stayed.'[53]

Manuel learned about RAV during a visit to his mother-in-law's house. According to his narrative, his mother-in-law was very ill, in her last days. 'When I arrived at her house, it was full of people', he said.[54] Many of these were members from RAV who were visiting the family. During the visit, Manuel asked his cousin who all these people were, and the cousin answered, 'It's my church, RAV'.[55] A couple of days after the death of his mother-in-law, Manuel and his family visited RAV, 'and it has been seven years since then'.[56]

Of all the interviewees, Pablo represents those whose arrival was not as pleasant as the rest. Pablo came to RAV almost two years prior to my visit. According to some of the congregants, it seems surreal to see Pablo worshiping with them. Pablo was the pastor of another Pentecostal church nearby. His story tells much about RAV's identity.

---

[51] Antonio. 2016. Focus group interview by author. Aguas Buenas, PR. July 3.
[52] Pedro. 2016. Focus group interview by author. Aguas Buenas, PR. July 3.
[53] Pedro. 2016. Focus group interview by author. Aguas Buenas, PR. July 3.
[54] Manuel. 2016. Focus group interview by author. Aguas Buenas, PR. July 3.
[55] Pedro. 2016. Focus group interview by author. Aguas Buenas, PR. July 3.
[56] Pedro. 2016. Focus group interview by author. Aguas Buenas, PR. July 3.

I come from a Pentecostal church that understood that *having any form of relationship with the world was to be in enmity with God*. My wife could not stand this type of teaching, so she left and decided to worship at RAV. My church believed that RAV was a *pelota de mundo* (a ball of worldliness), *because they described themselves as a church with open doors*. But there were three events that were transformative for me and that changed my understanding of RAV. The first two occurred during a Mother's Day service. Our children decided to go with their mom to RAV, and I did, too. First, when I arrived at the sanctuary, the presence of the Holy Spirit could be felt undeniably. The testimony of the Spirit was real. Second, as soon as he knew I was there, pastor Willy came up to me and said, 'We are honored to have you with us'. 'An honor!' I said to myself. After all I have said, that was really unexpected. But the third and final event was the exclamation point on the whole thing. One Sunday, my daughter asked me if I could go with her to RAV. As we were driving up to RAV, I told the Lord that regardless of the church where she became a follower of him, I would make that church my church. That day, my daughter accepted Christ at RAV.[57]

Knowing that some of the participants came from different Pentecostal experiences and that others had little or no experiences in Pentecostalism, I ended our session by asking them how RAV has informed their understanding of what it means to be church. Their responses were not only varied but also confirmed the integrative character that I had observed throughout their *cultos*.

Antonio was to the first to respond. He stated, 'What I learned here was the meaning of being *God's ambassadors to the world*'.[58] To be a Christian, he added, is to 'live for him and to work for him'.[59] Carmen underscored the integrative character of evangelism. 'We have to *preach the gospel with actions*. It is not only about offering prayers; we also have to give. We have to *preach the gospel with compassion*, just as Jesus did.'[60] Pedro focused on the element of the church with open

---

[57] Pablo. 2016. Focus group interview by author. Aguas Buenas, PR. July 3. Italics mine.

[58] Antonio. 2016. Focus group interview by author. Aguas Buenas, PR. July 3. Italics mine.

[59] Antonio. 2016. Focus group interview by author. Aguas Buenas, PR. July 3. Italics mine.

[60] Carmen. 2016. Focus group interview by author. Aguas Buenas, PR. July 3. Italic mine.

doors. RAV is a church that 'stresses the need to *be a church which is not enclosed*. We are a church with open doors.'[61] I followed up and asked Pedro if he could unpack what he meant by 'open doors'. He replied with a two-fold explanation. 'Open, because no one who comes to our community will be rejected. They come, and the Holy Spirit is the one who transforms all of us. And open, because we also go out. We intentionally participate in many public events. This church is part of the community.'[62] Pablo was the last to share his input. His answer offers a unique understanding of being church, and he raises the point about the importance of education in the local church. Pablo says,

> The church *is the voice of God*, and if she understands how to use this voice, the church will make a great impact. On the other hand, RAV takes time to train its members, and *through intentional education, we have learned what it means to be God's church*. In this church, I learned the integrative character of what it means to be holy and sanctified. RAV has attuned our senses to serve our communities.[63]

Following Pablo's answer, Antonio underscored the importance that education has played in constructing the public character of RAV members. 'As Pablo said, I understand that education is key in this whole process. We have become a church for the community because we have been taught to do so.'[64] In like manner, most of the younger adults also confirmed this. For example, reflecting on how RAV has impacted this understanding of the public realm, Ricardo said, 'RAV's intentional teachings help me understand the need to have an impact in the public sphere. Bible studies were central in transforming my way of thinking.'[65] In addition, and like Ricardo, María shared that 'RAV has been instrumental in teaching us the

---

[61] Pedro. 2016. Focus group interview by author. Aguas Buenas, PR. July 3. Italic mine.

[62] Pedro. 2016. Focus group interview by author. Aguas Buenas, PR. July 3. Italic mine.

[63] Pablo. 2016. Focus group interview by author. Aguas Buenas, PR. July 3. Italic mine.

[64] Antonio. 2016. Focus group interview by author. Aguas Buenas, PR. July 3. Italic mine.

[65] Ricardo. 2016. Focus group interview by author. Aguas Buenas, PR. June 26.

importance of going and impacting the public space. Our benediction reminds us to go and impact the public arena after every service.[66]

Church and Society

Once the focus group participants shared the context and their degree of involvement in RAV, we moved on to discuss how they understood the relationship of the church (in general) to society. The two guiding questions were the following: When you listen to the statement that there should be a division between church and society, what is your reaction? How do you describe RAV's involvement in public issues?

Regarding the first question, they all agreed that such division is difficult to understand and to maintain. For Antonio, both the church and society have utilized the 'wall' in different convenient circumstances. Yet 'RAV has been clear in teaching us that we are citizens, and we are encouraged to participate with all the rights that we have'.[67] Antonio was clear in stating that his beliefs do inform his decisions. Unfortunately, 'the Pentecostal church has been lax in educating her people to be part of the public and political discussion. Yet there has been a change in the mindset of Pentecostals, and through education we have become more aware of the importance of participating in public spheres.'[68] Pedro followed with a similar line of thought: 'It is difficult to separate one thing from the other (the church from society)'.[69] Pedro was emphatic in saying that RAV members are part of the state. According to his understanding, many churches have opted to be silent on public issues, but 'RAV has taken an alternate route. *We have learned to develop a public discourse.*'[70] He also added that integration is a must, but 'counter-culturally'.[71]

In addition, it is important to mention that Manuel made it clear that there is still much ground to cover. Interestingly, he understands that the social imaginary of Pentecostals and their reluctance to move into the public sphere might be connected to their eschatological fervency. 'It might be that the early experiences of our forefathers and

---

[66] María. 2016. Focus group interview by author. Aguas Buenas, PR. June 26.
[67] Antonio. 2016. Focus group interview by author. Aguas Buenas, PR. July 10.
[68] Antonio. 2016. Focus group interview by author. Aguas Buenas, PR. July 10.
[69] Pedro. 2016. Focus group interview by author. Aguas Buenas, PR. July 10.
[70] Pedro. 2016. Focus group interview by author. Aguas Buenas, PR. July 10.
[71] Pedro. 2016. Focus group interview by author. Aguas Buenas, PR. July 10.

foremothers have affected our political and public participation. Believing that he was coming soon, we have opted to stay looking inward.'[72] Pablo had a similar thought, using the teaching of sanctification. 'We see ourselves as so holy that we do not want to cross into the public realm.'[73] Instead of speaking up, 'we have stayed silent looking up, and not looking out to the public sphere'.[74]

From here, we went on to describe in what ways RAV has moved into public spaces. In general, the perception of the participants was that RAV seeks to connect in as many ways as possible, whether individually or as community.

Pedro's account is quite astonishing, to such an extent that he knows that some fellow members see his practice as too radical. He said,

> I told the pastor that I wanted to reach a community that is quite messy. If we do not go to them, they will not come to us. So, once a week I go to the bar and spent a couple of hours with the people that go to drink or play dominoes. I have earned their respect. And two have come to know Christ at the bar. See, there are places where the church needs to go, and we need to be there no matter what. As long as the Holy Spirit keeps pushing me there, I will be there.[75]

RAV is also active as a whole. On the one hand, Manuel recognizes that RAV has made intentional efforts to hold certain meetings outside of the sanctuary. For example, '*El viernes santo* (Good Friday) we use the town's basketball court and invite the whole community. This is probably the biggest gathering we have all year.'[76] On the other hand, Rebecca states that not all of RAV's gatherings out in the community are for the purpose of holding a *culto*. 'Some church members have battled cancer or have family members that have gone down that path, so pastors Willy and Miriam have made a firm effort to participate every year as sponsors and participants of *relevo por la vida* (an event hosted by the American Cancer Association).'[77] Being present in an event like this has opened their minds about the

[72] Manuel. 2016. Focus group interview by author. Aguas Buenas, PR. July 10.
[73] Pablo. 2016. Focus group interview by author. Aguas Buenas, PR. July 10.
[74] Pablo. 2016. Focus group interview by author. Aguas Buenas, PR. July 10.
[75] Pedro. 2016. Focus group interview by author. Aguas Buenas, PR. July 10.
[76] Manuel. 2016. Focus group interview by author. Aguas Buenas, PR. July 10.
[77] Rebecca. 2016. Focus group interview by author. Aguas Buenas, PR. June 26.

uncommon missionary avenues that the public sphere presents. Antonio confessed, 'The first time I heard that RAV was participating in *relevo por la vida*, I was shocked. But then I thought, wait a minute, this is good thing, we have to be there.'[78]

Theology/Liturgy

The last set of questions focused on the liturgy and its relation to the public sphere. The two questions discussed were, if possible, can you recognize what element(s) fuel(s) RAV's outward mission? How has your understanding of being Pentecostal contributed to the way you live your faith in your lived spaces?

Responses to the fueling elements were varied. For Manuel, RAV, as a community or represented by an individual, has learned that 'we do not need to be afraid of walking with those in need. The same transforming experience that we have received becomes a missional agent in us.'[79] For Pedro, RAV has an embedded missionary spirit. 'I understand that we go out, because once you become part of RAV, going out to serve the Other becomes part of your DNA.'[80] Furthermore, Antonio finds his fuel in his gratitude and in his obedience. 'By gratitude I mean that once you have received God's mercy and favor, you want to share with others such an experience. And by obedience, well, God has called us to love the world, as he did. Therefore, there are no excuses.'[81] Along with Antonio, Carmen mentions that compassion plays a major role in her point of view. 'Compassion makes us see things in light of how God sees us in Christ. Compassion fuels me to go out.'[82] Suddenly, Ricardo said, 'What about the pastors?'[83] 'What about them?', I replied. 'They also play a major role. I met them in a context outside of the church. And their actions made me understand that I had to do the same.'[84] Then, after a moment of silence, Antonio mentions that their responsibilities as citizens move them out as well. For example, he explains,

> one of my brothers from church, he works as a prison guard. He moves out to that place because that is part of his duty as an

---

[78] Antonio. 2016. Focus group interview by author. Aguas Buenas, PR. July 10.
[79] Manuel. 2016. Focus group interview by author. Aguas Buenas, PR. June 22.
[80] Pedro. 2016. Focus group interview by author. Aguas Buenas, PR. June 22.
[81] Antonio. 2016. Focus group interview by author. Aguas Buenas, PR. June 22.
[82] Carmen. 2016. Focus group interview by author. Aguas Buenas, PR. June 22.
[83] Pedro. 2016. Focus group interview by author. Aguas Buenas, PR. June 26.
[84] Pedro. 2016. Focus group interview by author. Aguas Buenas, PR. June 26.

employee. Yet when he goes, he understands that his faith experience goes with him. Through his lived testimony, he became acquainted with a convicted felon. When this man fulfilled his sentence, he decided to visit RAV, and ever since he has been part of our community.[85]

This testimony opened the way for the follow-up question of how their Pentecostal experience contributes to the way they live their faith in their lived spaces. Manuel, almost jumping up from his chair, said, 'Was not the Spirit moving over the Earth in Genesis? We are an incarnational church. Therefore, wherever we move, the Spirit is with us to be agents of change.'[86] For Luz, there is no way of dividing her faith experience from her lived space. 'My integrity is guided by my faith experience. If my lifestyle and decisions, even those that I make publicly, do not reflect the faith that I profess, then I am rejecting what I believe.'[87] In a similar way, María added, 'The reason I find the integration of both to be important is that, as Christians, we must come to our communities spiritually prepared, so that whatever we do or say may be consonant to the language of our faith'.[88]

Conclusion

This chapter demonstrates how religion, context, and the public sphere are integrated among Pentecostals in the Puerto Rican landscape. Moreover, recognizing that the locus of Pentecostal theology and spirituality lies in the *culto pentecostal* (Pentecostal worship service), the final section of this chapter described, by way of the implementation of ethnographic methodology, the close relationship that exists between lived faith and lived realities within one Pentecostal community.

Before moving to the following chapter, I would like to reveal some findings that are key to the study and at the same time highlight overlooked understandings regarding the relationship between church and society within the Puerto Rican context. For example, it seems that Puerto Rican religiosity, and Pentecostalism being one

---

[85] Antonio. 2016. Focus group interview by author. Aguas Buenas, PR. June 22.
[86] Manuel. 2016. Focus group interview by author. Aguas Buenas, PR. June 22.
[87] Luz. 2016. Focus group interview by author. Aguas Buenas, PR. June 26.
[88] María. 2016. Focus group interview by author. Aguas Buenas, PR. June 26.

among them, though very much impacted by Western understandings of Christianity through colonization and foreign missionary endeavors, has maintained, in contrast, a wholistic and a fluid relationship between the sacred and the public. This integrative character, rather than an expression of Western ecclesiology, stands against it and affirms the religious undercurrent heritage of indigenous and African spiritualties which are very much present today.[89] Furthermore, and in connection to the previous, it seems that RAV demonstrates such a fluid relationship. For them the church is not a place beyond the public. The church, though a distinct community called by God, is placed in the midst of this world as a re-imagined community, not for the sake of themselves, but for all. As a result, whatever they do as church community has implications for society as a whole. Therefore, liturgy or el *culto* is not only the work of the people, but also the work for the people beyond the church community.

How these findings contribute to a lived ecclesiology? The results of this case study, along with the work of the theologians in Chapter 3, will be central to the construction of a Pentecostal lived ecclesiology, which is the focus of the following chapter.

---

[89] Not all theology or spirituality occurs *above ground*, due to oppression or persecution some theological and spiritual expression choose or are pushed *underground*. Nevertheless, these underground currents play a significant role in transforming the religious landscape just as those that stay above. See Paul R Spickard and Kevin M. Cragg, *A Gobal History of Christians: How Everyday Believers Experienced Their World* (Grand Rapids, MI: Baker Books, 2001), p. 375.

5

CONSTRUCTING A PENTECOSTAL LIVED ECCLESIOLOGY

Lived Faith and Lived Realities in Conversation

What has been said up to this point? I have argued that the question of Pentecostalism and the public space is both a theological and an anthropological question. My testimony illustrated the experiential character that was modeled in the intimacy of my home and then as part of a Pentecostal community. The theological aspect of the question has to do with the way Pentecostal faith occurs as a part of public life. Such an inquiry is not new, but there needs to be an ongoing revision, taking into consideration new local questions and present realities.[1] Consequently, this study called for an interdisciplinary framework and methodology. The framework has been sustained through a trialectical relationship between Pentecostal, contextual, and public theologies (Chapter 1). In addition, the methodology sought to integrate the literature-based research (Chapter 3) with an empirical study (Chapter 4). Chapter 3 examined the theological contributions of three Latino/a Pentecostal theologians who underscored the intrinsic relationship between theology, the church, and

---

[1] I have to underscore Robert Schreiter's call for 'new questions' as central for Latin American Christianity. Much of the gospel received from foreign missionaries to Latin America was a transplant of what they had experienced in the North. Thus, the opportunity to (re)think and (re)discover the gospel through new questions is key for Latin American theology. This shift will develop a unique theological discourse, which can contribute to the global Christian body. See, for example, Robert J. Schreiter, *Constructing Local Theologies* (Maryknoll, NY: Orbis Books, 1985).

the public space. They recognized the personal and public implications of the baptism of the Holy Spirit. However, they also made clear that there is much to be done with the latter and challenged the Pentecostal community to recall her public character as a response from theological conviction. Hence, according to these theologians, Pentecostal churches must work to bring down the wall between private and public when it comes to theology. In the preceding chapter, priority was given to the local experiences that occur in *el culto pentecostal* (the Pentecostal worship service).[2] Through the implementation of ethnographic methods such as participant observation and focus group interviews, it was established that within *el culto pentecostal* there is an overlapping relationship between the lived faith and the lived realities of the people. Paraphrasing those who participated, there is an interconnectivity between the fullness of the Spirit and the public character of the Pentecostal community.[3]

Now that the foundation has been laid, this chapter will attempt the construction of a Pentecostal lived ecclesiology. The theological construction proposed herein is not only concerned with content but also with method.[4] For that reason, though the methodology of how the study was conducted was presented in the first chapter, there are some specifics regarding Pentecostal theological method that need to be further unpacked as part of the contributions of this study. Then, following this methodological proposal, the chapter moves toward the construction of a Pentecostal lived ecclesiology that surfaces from the dialogue between praxis and theory.

---

[2] Speaking about the 'local' in the task of 'doing theology', Sedmak mentions that to be local, any theological argument 'must be rooted in a local culture'. See Clemens Sedmak, *Doing Local Theology: A Guide for Artisans of a New Humanity* (Faith and Cultures Series; Maryknoll, NY: Orbis Books, 2002).

[3] See Chapter 3.

[4] Though the experience of Pentecost is by nature contextual, there has been little conversation about a Pentecostal contextual model or method. Accordingly, most of the literature that I have read concerning the topic of method and model in contextual theology is silent about the proposal that Pentecostals bring to the topic. See, for example, A. Scott Moreau, 'Evangelical Models of Contextualization', in Matthew Cook (ed.), *Local Theology for the Global Church: Principles for an Evangelical Approach to Contextualization* (Pasadena: World Evangelical Alliance Theological Commission, 2010), Kindle loc. 5847.

A Pentecostal Method for a Lived Ecclesiology: An Exploration

The discussion of Pentecostal method involves an array of voices from within and outside the Pentecostal movement. These voices may be categorized into two overarching groups. In one, we find those who understand that using terms such as 'Pentecostal', 'theology', and 'method' in the same sentence is a trifle-like dessert: i.e. ingredients that do not blend well together.[5] A subsection of this group are voices that recognize some sort of Pentecostal overtones, but are guided by non-Pentecostal methodologies. In other words, the work of the Holy Spirit is understood as an *additivus* to Evangelical theological thought. The second overarching group is represented by voices which affirm that Pentecostals bring a unique contribution to the discussion of theological method.[6] In the words of James K.A. Smith, '[Pentecostalism is] not anti-intellectual in the sense that it is opposed to academic research or critical inquiry'; on the contrary, Pentecostals bring an 'integral Pentecostal scholarship' that is unique from Evangelicalism.[7]

Personally, I locate myself in the group that finds within Pentecostalism the biblical, historical, theological, and spiritual depth to contribute to the conversation about theological method. And regardless of arriving late to the methodological *fiesta* (feast), this does not mean that we are only responsible for just a simple side dish.[8] I can say this today because I am standing on the shoulders of women

---

[5] See, for example, Mark A. Noll, *The Scandal of the Evangelical Mind* (Grand Rapids, MI: Eerdmans, 1995). In this book, representative of an era that wanted to 'save' the Evangelical mind from theological digression, Noll accuses Pentecostalism and like-minded movements of ostracizing the Evangelical mind and portrays them as scandalous.

[6] However, it is important to recognize that there is still no uniformity within this group. For example, some consider that the unique contribution Pentecostals can make is skewed. In his review of Christopher Stephenson's work on Pentecostal theological methods, Wolfgang Vondey states, 'Stephenson's suggestion that Pentecostals are becoming more attentive to theological method is perhaps more wishful thinking than current reality'. See Wolfgang Vondey, 'Types of Pentecostal Theology: Method, System, Spirit', *Pneuma (Online)* 37.1 (2015), pp. 160–62. Also see Christopher A. Stephenson, *Types of Pentecostal Theology: Method, System, Spirit*, Academy Series (New York: Oxford University Press, 2013).

[7] James K.A. Smith, 'Scandalizing Theology: A Pentecostal Response to Noll's Scandal', *Pneuma* 19.2 (September 1997), pp. 232–33.

[8] See Terry L. Cross, 'The Rich Feast of Theology: Can Pentecostals Bring the Main Course or Only the Relish?', *Journal of Pentecostal Theology* 8.16 (April 2000), pp. 27–47.

and men who paved the way for future Pentecostal scholarship. The first generation of Pentecostal scholars did not study in institutions that were Pentecostal in orientation; thus, though their content was Pentecostal in nature, it was guided by methods and forms that were not.[9] However, these scholars laid the foundation over which future generations began to develop both the content and the method of Pentecostal theology within newly established Pentecostal educational institutions.[10] Hence, what is our contribution to the *fiesta*? What follows, rather than exhaustive, is a representative list[11] that not only serves as a testimony of the contributions of Pentecostals to the methodological discussion but is also a platform on which a Pentecostal public method could be based.

Pentecostals and Theological Method

No discussion on Pentecostal theology can begin without mentioning the seminal work of Steven J. Land. Perhaps one of the first major works that revealed the paradigm shift that was erupting among Pentecostal scholarship is Land's *Pentecostal Spirituality*.[12] In this monograph, Land makes a courageous attempt to interpret and revise the Pentecostal tradition by analyzing 'belief and practices as integrated in the affections – showing the crucial role played by eschatology'.[13] For Land, eschatology is a central lens for the Pentecostal theological approach. He states,

> Since Pentecostalism is an apocalyptic movement of the Spirit, it will want to have the eschatological context and horizon prominently displayed in a theological approach which is not only a reflection *upon*, but a reflection *of* and *within* reality. What was implicit

---

[9] See Thomas, 'Pentecostal Theology in the Twenty-First Century'.

[10] It is important to establish that just as there are many Pentecostalisms, there is no unified Pentecostal method in the movement. Consequently, though the examples presented have impacted the Pentecostal movement, they are more closely related to the 'Cleveland school of thought'. Cleveland school of thought is a very recent terminology that is applicable to Pentecostal scholars that are connected or impacted by the Pentecostal Theological Seminary.

[11] Yet, for those interested in researching more about Pentecostals and method, see Stephenson, *Types of Pentecostal Theology*. Stephenson presents one of the first (if not the first) monographs that studies the contribution of Pentecostals to theological method.

[12] Land, *Pentecostal Spirituality*, p. 1. By spirituality he means, 'the integration of beliefs and practices, in the affections which are themselves evoked and expressed by those beliefs and practices'.

[13] Land, *Pentecostal Spirituality*, p. 17.

in Pentecostal history and thought must now be made explicit, but cast in a different way.[14]

Furthermore, important in Land's proposal is the role of spirituality, theology, and method.[15] For Land, there is a distinct Pentecostal 'relationship between theology and spirituality'.[16] This relationship is revealed in the affections of the person and the community. These affections are not mere subjective and feeble emotions but are 'the existential core of faith', and, thus, central 'for the whole theological enterprise'.[17] In short, it is a theological model located in the 'apocalyptic affections' (i.e. experiences) of Pentecostals.[18] The importance of Land's contribution stands in that he, along with other Pentecostal scholars, paved the way for the uniqueness of a Pentecostal approach. This uniqueness is rooted in the Pentecostal *experience*.

Another methodological model proposed by Pentecostals takes into consideration the fivefold gospel paradigm.[19] This paradigm affirms Christ as Savior, Sanctifier, Spirit Baptizer, Healer, and Coming King.[20] During his 1998 presidential address at the Society of Pentecostal Studies (SPS), New Testament scholar John Christopher Thomas proposed a Pentecostal theology which is rooted within this

---

[14] Steven J. Land, 'A Passion for the Kingdom: Revisioning Pentecostal Spirituality', *Journal of Pentecostal Theology* 1.1 (1992), p. 28.

[15] Land, *Pentecostal Spirituality*, p. 15.

[16] Land, *Pentecostal Spirituality*, p. 1.

[17] Harvey Cox, 'A Review of 'Pentecostal Spirituality: A Passion for the Kingdom', by Steven J Land', *Journal of Pentecostal Theology* 5 (October 1994), p. 4.

[18] Cox, 'A Review of 'Pentecostal Spirituality', p. 4.

[19] See 'The Question of Pentecostalism' under the Theoretical Framework section in chapter 1 for a word on the development of the fivefold gospel.

[20] Though I am referring specifically to the use of the fivefold pattern, it is important to mention that not all Pentecostals adhere to this paradigm. It has been established historically and theologically that within Pentecostalism there are two fourfold patterns. On the one hand, some affirm Christ as Savior, Sanctifier, Healer, and Coming King. On the other hand, some affirm Christ as Savior, Spirit Baptizer, Healer, and Coming King. For a brief explanation of the nuances of these patterns, see the Theoretical Framework section in Chapter 1. Also, I recommend the following readings: Donald W. Dayton, *Theological Roots of Pentecostalism* (Peabody, MA: Hendrickson Pub., 1987); Vinson Synan, *The Holiness-Pentecosal Tradition: Charismatic Movements in the Twentieth Century* (Grand Rapids, MI: Eerdmans, 2nd edn, 1997); Kenneth J. Archer, *A Pentecostal Hermeneutic: Spirit, Scripture, and Community* (2004; repr., Cleveland, TN: CPT Press, 2009); Allan Anderson, *Spreading Fires: The Missionary Nature of Early Pentecostalism* (Maryknoll, NY: Orbis Books, 2007); Vinson Synan, *The Century of Holy Spirit: 100 Years of Pentecostal and Charismatic Renewal, 1901–2001* (Nashville: Thomas Nelson, 2012).

fivefold gospel.[21] Consequently, he challenged the audience to consider the idea of constructing a theology from within and invited them to articulate 'a theology that is distinctively Pentecostal'.[22] Such an invitation lies within the following premise: 'the theological heart of Pentecostalism is the fivefold gospel'; hence, 'when a Pentecostal theology is written from the ground up, it will be structured around these central tenets of Pentecostal faith and preaching'.[23] One who followed Thomas's proposal was Kenneth Archer. The following quote explains succinctly the importance of this theological method:

> Thus the Five-fold Gospel is not a set of quaint platitudes but deep-seated, affectionate affirmations flowing from our worship of the living God who has transformed our lives ... For Pentecostals, then, our story with its central narrative convictions expressed through the Five-fold Gospel needs to take on a more overt role in our theological explanations. One important way of articulating a Pentecostal theology then would be to shape it around our story and structure it around the Five-fold Gospel.[24]

The importance of this proposal is that it takes into consideration the way that early Pentecostals understood Christ's salvific work.[25] Therefore, this method is framed by a Spirit-christology where Christ is revealed as Sammy Alfaro coined, our *Divino Compañero*, a 'divine

---

[21] See Thomas, 'Pentecostal Theology in the Twenty-First Century'.

[22] Thomas, 'Pentecostal Theology in the Twenty-First Century', p. 17.

[23] Thomas, 'Pentecostal Theology in the Twenty-First Century', p. 17. As examples of works that use this theological method, see Archer, *A Pentecostal Hermeneutic*; John Christopher Thomas (ed.), *Toward a Pentecostal Ecclesiology: The Church and the Fivefold Gospel* (Cleveland, TN: CPT Press, 2010); Amos Yong, *In the Days of Caesar: Pentecostalism and Political Theology* (The Cadbury Lectures 2009; Grand Rapids, MI: Eerdmans, 2010).

[24] Archer, *A Pentecostal Hermeneutic*, pp. 312–13, adds:

> The theological center is the person Jesus Christ, and protruding out of the center are the five spokes which serve to explain the significance of the story of Jesus Christ for the community and the world ... Our Pentecostal doctrinal practices and beliefs are the wheel, connected to and stabilized by the spokes, yet turning and spinning around its center – Jesus Christ. Pentecostal beliefs and practices, therefore, will always flow back to their center where they find their ultimate significance and justification – Jesus Christ.

[25] Interestingly, this theme is not only prevalent in early North American Pentecostalism, as is argued by many Pentecostal scholars, but this paradigm is also present in the newspapers, letters, testimonies, songs, and sermons from my Puerto Rican Pentecostal foremothers and fathers. See Estrada, *El fuego está encendido*.

companion' in our salvific journey.[26] For Thomas, Archer, Alfaro, and other scholars, early Pentecostal literature affirms such a paradigm and therefore should not be overlooked in discussions of a Pentecostal approach (or 'method') to theologizing.

In addition, Pentecostal scholars also contributed the trialectical[27] method of Spirit-Word-Community.[28] Though it began as a biblical-hermeneutical method,[29] Pentecostal theologians like Amos Yong[30] have adopted it as a theological framework. The theological approach, according to Yong, is infused by 'the perichoretic indwelling of the inter-Trinitarian relationships'.[31] In other words, just as there is an *intimate union* between all three Persons of the Godhead, there is an analogous relationship among the Spirit-Word-Community. For Yong, the theological enterprise is a lively progression where the task of theology is both theoretical and practical. Through this trialectical theological approach, the theologian embarks on a task in which there is an integral interpretation of all human actions. Also helpful to this method is the liberty of the theologian to begin from any of the three hermeneutical axels. Regardless of the starting point, they will meet, confront, and inform each other. In his review of Yong's proposal, William Oliverio underscores that the contribution of Yong lies in that he 'offers a constructive effort at theological hermeneutics, boldly forging a holistic vision which develops ontology,

---

[26] Sammy Alfaro, *Divino Compañero: Toward a Hispanic Pentecostal Christology* (Eugene, OR: Wipf & Stock, 2010).

[27] It is trialectical in that these three moments are interstructurally given, interdependent, interconnected, interrelated, interpenetrating and interinfluential, and reciprocal. Amos Yong, 'The Hermeneutical Trialectic: Notes Toward a Consensual Hermeneutic and Theological Method', *Heythrop Journal* 45.1 (January 2004), p. 23.

[28] Among these scholars I can mention the contributions of John Christopher Thomas, Amos Yong, and Kenneth Archer.

[29] See Thomas, John Christopher, 'Women, Pentecostalism and the Bible: An Experiment in Pentecostal Hermeneutics', *Journal of Pentecostal Theology* 5 (1994), pp. 41-56, and John Christopher Thomas, 'Reading the Bible from within Our Traditions: A Pentecostal Hermeneutic as a Test Case', in Joel B. Green and Max Turner, (eds.), *Between Two Horizons: Spanning New Testament Studies and Systematic Theology* (Grand Rapids, MI: Eerdmans, 1999), pp. 108–22.

[30] Amos Yong, *Spirit, Word, Community: Theological Hermeneutics in Trinitarian Perspective* (Eugene, OR: Wipf & Stock, 2006).

[31] Furthermore, Yong explains that though he is not the first to use a model analogous to the inter-Trinitarian relationship, what is missing from other proposals is 'a robust pneumatology to sustain the triadic movement' where '[n]one operate apart from the other two'. Yong, 'The Hermeneutical Trialectic', p. 22.

metaphysics, epistemology and hermeneutics together into an account of what theologically interpreting the world entails'.[32] The contribution of this model is in highlighting the integrative character of Pentecostals in the task of theological and cultural interpretation.

Furthermore, Pentecostals have constructed their theological thought considering the relationship of orthodoxy, orthopathy, and orthopraxis. In the article 'A Pentecostal Way of Doing Theology: Method and Manner', Kenneth Archer suggests such an approach.[33] Contrary to Western philosophical tradition, instead of beginning with theory, Pentecostal methodology is more faithful to its nature when it begins with *praxis*. Affirming the work of Jackie and Cheryl Bridges Johns,[34] Archer explains, 'Instead of theory leading to practice, theory becomes, or is seen in, the reflective moment in praxis'.[35] From this perspective 'theory arises from praxis to wield further praxis'.[36] Thus praxis (orthopraxis) takes us into knowing (orthodoxy). Yet, Archer affirms the importance of another integrative component to praxis and knowing, that is suffering, or affections (depending on who defines it). Drinking from the well of Latino Pentecostal theologian Samuel Solivan,[37] Archer proposes that orthopathos (*right suffering* for Solivan) is important because, first, orthopathy safeguards us from a theology that is detached from the concrete realities of suffering that much of those in the world, especially the Majority World, are experiencing. Second, orthopathy provides a necessary

---

[32] L. William Oliverio, Jr., 'An Interpretive Review Essay on Amos Yong's Spirit-Word-Community: Theological Hermeneutics in Trinitarian Perspective', *Journal of Pentecostal Theology* 18.2 (2009), p. 302.

[33] Kenneth J. Archer, 'A Pentecostal Way of Doing Theology: Method and Manner', *International Journal of Systematic Theology* 9.3 (July 2007), pp. 301–14. I must add that presently, Archer is expanding his approach. In a recent presentation, he affirmed the 'integration of orthopistis (right belief), and orthopraxis (right action) and orthopathos (holy affection)'. Yet, he also stated that these three are interconnected to 'orthodoxy (right worship), orthomartus (right witness) and orthoergon (right work)'. For now, we must wait for his complete proposal. Kenneth Archer, 'A Global Pentecostal Methodology: Worship, Witness, and Work', presented at the III International Seminar on Pentecostals, Theology, and the Sciences of Sao Paulo (UMESP) in Sao Paulo, Brazil.

[34] Jackie David Johns and Cheryl Bridges Johns, 'Yielding to the Spirit: A Pentecostal Approach to Group Bible Study', *Journal of Pentecostal Theology* 1.1 (1992), pp. 109–34.

[35] Archer, 'A Pentecostal Way of Doing Theology', p. 309.

[36] Archer, 'A Pentecostal Way of Doing Theology', p. 309.

[37] Samuel Solivan, *The Spirit, Pathos and Liberation: Toward a Hispanic Pentecostal Theology* (JPTSup 14; Sheffield: Sheffield Academic Press, 1998).

corrective to the narrower conservative modernistic view of orthodoxy as correct propositional truth claims. In other words, 'orthopathos puts us in touch with the compassionate redemptive liberation
of Jesus Christ and the Holy Spirit'.[38] Moreover, says Solivan,

> Orthopathos, as an epistemological resource for theology, can as-
> sist the theologian to bridge the gap between critical reflection and
> interpersonal engagement … [Orthopathos] seeks to affirm the
> important contribution that personal experience can have on crit-
> ical theological formation and dialogue.[39]

What I find interesting about this approach is that it takes the context
seriously. Praxis and theory need to be grounded in those it is geared
for; if not, it fails to respond to the realities of the people.

Finally, I want to mention the contribution of Terry Cross.[40] Cross
has been an advocate for the uniqueness of Pentecostal theology and
method. Unfortunately, so far Cross has not written a monograph on
this topic, but he has published various articles that speak to it. Of
his articles, two are useful for this study. In the first, 'The Rich Feast
of Theology: Can Pentecostals Bring the Main Course or Only the
Relish?' Cross responds to Clark Pinnock's invitation to Pentecostals
to be part of the theological feast.[41] In the second, 'A Proposal to
Break the Ice: What Can Pentecostal Theology Offer Evangelical
Theology', Cross challenges Evangelical theology to leave its strict
'rationalistic approach' and learn from its Pentecostal brothers and
sisters, new avenues of theological engagement. Central to both articles is Cross's understanding that *experience* plays a central role in the
process of doing Pentecostal theology. Cross affirms, 'Because we
know and *experience* God in the existential *reality* of our lives, we are
prepared to construct our theological understanding of God with

---

[38] Archer, 'A Pentecostal Way of Doing Theology', p. 310.

[39] He adds, 'The polarization of orthodoxy and orthopraxis has been detri-
mental to the poor and the suffering who often find that they must choose between
their piety and their socio-political survival'. Solivan, *The Spirit, Pathos and Liberation*,
p. 37.

[40] Rather than exhaustive, this section is representative of the development of
Pentecostal methodology. To date, there is only one monograph that seeks to study
the contribution of Pentecostalism to theological method. Yet Stephenson's contribution is also a representative work of a larger discussion. See Stephenson, *Types
of Pentecostal Theology*.

[41] See Cross, 'The Rich Feast of Theology'.

this experiential reality in mind'.[42] In other words, God's relationality, rather than a hindrance to theological method, is the central axis from which Pentecostals construct their theological understanding. Moreover, Cross is not oblivious to the challenges that Pentecostalism may confront as a relatively new movement on the block, yet he is aware that since the eighties Pentecostals have begun a trend that cannot be ignored. In response to critics, he states the following:

> Pentecostal theology can offer some suggestive avenues for approaching doctrine in today's world, but only if we are allowed (I understand that no permission is needed) to reflect on the ways we experience God and then offer that reflection as an important basis for our theology.[43]

What is helpful in Cross's argument is that Pentecostal theology, though it emphasizes experience (not to the exclusion of Scripture, tradition, or reason), is concerned with existential realities, takes many forms, and has different starting points. As he states, 'This diverse and immense movement is not characterized by one single theological method or reflection'.[44] Consequently, Pentecostal theologians have used distinct Pentecostal experiences such as the eschaton, Spirit baptism, tongue speaking, altar, and *coritos* (Pentecostal songs) as their methodological hubs.[45] The relationality of God with us opens many ways of engaging the methodological question.

I understand that each of the models above has a unique lens, yet these methods also underscore important elements for the task at hand. First, while implicit in the proposals, I cannot avoid beginning by pointing out that each method takes seriously the agency of the Holy Spirit and the profitableness of Scripture for the task of doing theology. It is only because of the work of the Spirit and Word in Pentecostals and in their worshiping communities that each of the

---

[42] Cross, 'The Rich Feast of Theology', p. 30. Emphasis added.

[43] Terry L Cross, 'A Proposal to Break the Ice: What Can Pentecostal Theology Offer Evangelical Theology?', *Journal of Pentecostal Theology* 10.2 (April 2002), p. 49.

[44] Cross, 'A Proposal to Break the Ice', p. 47.

[45] By 'distinct' I do not mean that they are nonexistent in other Christian movements; I mean their distinctiveness due to their adaptation to Pentecostal spirituality. For example, see Frank D Macchia, *Bautizado en el espíritu: una teología, pentecostal global* (Miami, FL: Vida, 2008); Wolfgang Vondey, 'The Making of a Black Liturgy: Pentecostal Worship and Spirituality from African Slave Narratives to American Cityscapes', *Black Theology* 10.2 (August 2012), pp. pp. 147–68; Alfaro, *Divino Compañero*.

previous methodologies has developed.[46] Second, these models spring from the forms/ways that Pentecostals embody their relationship to God. In other words, for them, theology is a way of life.[47] Third, and connected to the previous points, such a praxis is informed by the realities and *sufferings* of the individual and the community. By 'suffering' I am not only pointing to what has been stated above by Solivan, but also, to the suffering (the undergoing of pain) of what it means to comprehend God integrally, even if that full knowledge comes after an all-night struggle with God's angel or, as the apostle Paul says, through a dimmed mirror. Fourth, each of the models takes into consideration the importance of the community. However, this community seems to be bounded to the Christian and the Pentecostal communities, whether from the early church, local churches, or the academy. The question of how these methods are impacting those beyond this 'bounded set' is yet to be seen.[48] Fifth and finally, these models are rooted in context. They do not only arise from a specific place and time but also from personal experiences that seek to engage and contribute to the greater Pentecostal and Christian communities.

Constructing A Pentecostal Lived Ecclesiology: A Prolegomena

The task at hand is to construct a theological approach that integrates faith and the public sphere. I will begin by highlighting the important themes that surfaced from the empirical research discussed in Chapter 4. Then these findings will be analyzed alongside the contributions from Luvis, Villafañe, and Rodríguez.

---

[46] For example, reflecting on the centrality of the Holy Spirit for his theological task, Yong, 'The Hermeneutical Trialectic', p. 27, states,

Herein we are led into the heart of the Trinitarian mystery, yet one that is pneumatologically understood as the 'communion of the Holy Spirit' (2 Cor. 13:13). I was beginning to sense that a properly Pentecostal hermeneutic and theological method could and would indeed be pneumatologically driven, but that such a pneumatological starting point should not lapse into a mere pneumatocentrism but ought to be both Christomorphic and patromorphic at the same time.

[47] As James K.A. Smith calls it, 'Pentecostal spirituality is "a form of life"'. See James K.A. Smith, *Thinking in Tongues: Pentecostal Contributions to Christian Philosophy* (Pentecostal Manifestos; Grand Rapids, MI: Eerdmans, 2010), Kindle, 256.

[48] For an explanation of the elements as bounded and center sets, see Paul G. Hiebert, 'The category "Christian" in the Mission Task', *International Review of Mission* 72.287 (July 1983), pp. 421–27.

Conversion: From and To

Along with the doctrine of the Holy Spirit, soteriology (and conversion specifically) is another important doctrine among Pentecostals. As a matter of fact, as I grew up it was common for me to hear the refrain, *the power of the Holy Spirit able to convert us from this world*. However, this transformation only considered the individual's soul and being ransomed from the work of the devil.[49] As Kärkkäinen states, 'Pentecostals emphasize the changing of individuals whom, when formed into a body of believers, bring change into the culture from within'.[50] In response, some may be concerned about such a simplistic view of conversion.[51] Yet, as explained below, RAV Church witnessed an expanded understanding of conversion.

Those who experienced the before-and-after of the arrival of pastors Miriam and Willy to RAV recognized that the church went through a major transformation regarding her sensibility to the intersection of faith and life, of the sacred and the public. Prior to their arrival, RAV had a skewed view of the world (the public space). That is to say, the public space was understood as a place from which God is saving us; thus, why should Christians have any part of it?

To become a local church attuned to the public realm, RAV underwent a multilevel conversion process. The first conversion was the identity of the church. The previous name, *Barriada Vázquez* Church, had a very limited scope in terms of identity and mission. *Barriada Vázquez* is the name of a dead-end street with little to no impact in the city. Actually, for pastors Miriam and Willy, moving the church from that street to seven acres of open field became a sign of future hope for the church and the community; from the restraints of a dead end to the hope of a city on a hill. Moreover, such a conversion, which may seem superficial in a certain way, became the seedbed for a second conversion: a fresh missional infusion. Hence, it can be stated that when an individual or a community experiences an integral conversion, along with it come new forms of missional approaches.

---

[49] For example, see Dale M. Coulter, 'Baptism, Conversion, and Grace: Reflections on the "Underlying Realities" between Pentecostals, Methodists, and Catholics', *Pneuma* 31.2 (2009), pp. 189–212.

[50] Veli-Matti Kärkkäinen, *Toward a Pneumatological Theology: Pentecostal and Ecumenical Perspectives on Ecclesiology, Soteriology, and Theology of Mission* (Lanham, MD: University Press of America, 2002), p. 209.

[51] See the chapter on 'Culture, Contextualization and Conversion' in Kärkkäinen, *Toward a Pneumatological Theology*.

In other words, RAV was not only a proper name and an adjective for this local church, it also became a verb. The streams of living water became their DNA and source of being as a local community. In this concept, they reclaimed a common characteristic with the city of Aguas Buenas (Good Waters) and also appropriated their mission as a Pentecostal church. Another important conversion experience was RAV's (re)definition of her Pentecostal spirituality and theology. In response to the skewed view of the public sphere, pastors Willie and Miriam realized that to *be* Pentecostal should not just make us run *from* the world *to* God but also should make them run back *toward* the world in the power of the Holy Spirit with the Good News of the kingdom. For RAV, to *be* Pentecostal is to be committed to all areas of life.

Luvis, Villafañe, and López have a similar understanding. For example, for Luvis, to be in Christ in the power of the Holy Spirit must move us back *into* the world. *Está prohibido olvidar* (you must not forget) the place from which God had called you.[52] This call to remember where we were when God's grace reached us emphasizes not only the grace that has been given to us but also the need to go back and share with others the fruits of such grace. To cite Luvis, 'To be Pentecostal is … to concretize this reflection in a praxis that affirms the grace of being gifted'.[53] In addition, Villafañe underscores that as we are being called by God and baptized in the Spirit, we are free to move *into* and *from* the world as the Holy Spirit freely moves over us, in us, and through us. Moreover, for López, an individual or a community that has responded to God's call and has experienced the freedom that is given by the Holy Spirit should not create bifurcations between the church and the public space because 'God's purposes point to the reconciliation of all'.[54]

As mentioned above, conversion is the result of God's mission in this world. To paraphrase Orlando Costas, conversion is an invitation from God to all people.[55] God is inviting all humanity to enter into an eternal loving covenant. Moreover, conversion is not just an invitation. It is also a demand. Because of the demands at play in such an ongoing process, there is no neutral zone in the conversion event.

---

[52] It is forbidden to forget.
[53] Luvis, 'Sewing a New Cloth', p. 184.
[54] López, *Pentecostalismo y misión integral,* p. 12.
[55] Costas, *The Integrity of Mission,* p. 8.

There is a transformation that must take place in the life of the person who accepts the invitation. Costas says, 'The gospel *demands* a change of values and attitudes as a fundamental condition for participation in the life of the kingdom'.[56]

Frank Macchia stresses that conversion is not an *us* against *them* confrontation,[57] but it is 'the activity of God in the world to liberate and to redeem the creation'.[58] Hence, conversion is not a God event bounded only to the sacred but directed to the whole created order, and that includes the public sphere. Additionally, conversion to Christ must not alienate us from the Other; rather, conversion must make us more sensitive to the Other. If conversion is a person's turning to Christ and the beginning of a journey to become more like him, then there is also an implicit turning to the Other and to the spheres that are in need of Christ's presence. In the words of Macchia, 'Conversion should bring about humility, critical self-evaluation, and openness to the Other to see what God would teach us about the expanding horizon of the Kingdom of God in the world'.[59] In other words, to experience conversion is to become God's people for the world, as Jesus did in the power of the Holy Spirit.

---

[56] Orlando E. Costas, *The Integrity of Mission*, p. 8. Furthermore, conversion has various levels. Costas is known for his three-conversion process. This first can be described as his 'religious conversion'. That is, a person's response to God's call. The second level refers to his 'cultural conversion'. Through his new life in Christ he found himself as Puerto Rican and Latin American. In other words, to be called into God's triune relationship does not distance us from our societal and cultural realities. This second level was central to his theological methodology. And finally, the third level refers to his 'sociopolitical conversion'. He understood the centrality that the poor and the marginalized had in God's kingdom. Thus, there is a responsibility to engage the public. These three levels of conversion are not isolated events, but overlapping and continuous.

[57] Macchia states, 'Rather than an individualistic claim on having been awakened in distinction from those who have not, we should strive instead to reach for a more holistic and process oriented understanding of conversion that sees conversion as both an event and a process in which one journeys with others towards greater understanding of what it means to follow Christ in the world'. Frank D. Macchia, 'Towards Individual and Communal Renewal: Reflections on Luke's Theology of Conversion', *Ex Auditu* 25 (2009), p. 94.

[58] Macchia, 'Towards Individual and Communal Renewal', p. 93.

[59] Macchia, 'Towards Individual and Communal Renewal', p. 103. Elsewhere he states, 'The goal is that the people of God might then become the church for others in the world', p. 104.

An Integral Spirituality

A second theme that surfaced throughout my observations and the interviews with RAV members is the integration of practice and belief. Hence, an ecclesiology seeking to become public must affirm such an integral character. I could grasp, from their liturgy and interviews, that members of RAV sought to live a life in which faith and practices were congruent. Particularly, they took great care to explain how their experiences in the Holy Spirit shaped their actions. One of the youth leaders made this clear when she affirmed that her integrity is guided by her Pentecostal experience. Her decisions and actions must be harmonious to the faith that she believes; 'if not, I am a hypocrite'.[60] Affirming this integral character, another leader mentioned that our embodied language in the public sphere must be congruent with our faith language.[61] An example of this is Pedro's account of going back to the nearby bar and invest time with a group of men who spend their life drinking. This is, according to Pedro, how he integrates belief and practice, the sacred with the public. For each of those interviewed, our practices must serve as icons that point to our beliefs, and, likewise, our beliefs must point to our practices.

Similarly, all three Pentecostal theologians studied in Chapter 3 affirm the integral character of Pentecostal spirituality and theology. According to them, the relationship of faith and practice is seminal in the life of the Pentecostal community. Luvis affirms that the fabric of the new ecclesiological cloth that she wants to sew is developed from an intentional knitting of faith and practice. For her, this integration of character happens within *el culto* (the worship service). Likewise, Villafañe raises this issue of the centrality of faith and practice. In consent with Luvis, he also affirms that the locus of Pentecostal theology and spirituality is the worship service (*el culto*). However, this character is not only affirmed in words but also with deeds. As an example, Villafañe raises the theme of love. Accordingly, Villafañe's Spirit-ethic is rooted in the church's faculty to love God and love the Other. Love, in his understanding, has no worth or impact if it is not embodied as God embodied it through the sending-out-of-love, his only begotten son Jesus. Furthermore, Villafañe is emphatic in stating that among the areas that Pentecostals need to keep

---

[60] Luz. 2016. Focus group interview by author. Aguas Buenas, PR. June 26.
[61] María. 2016. Focus group interview by author. Aguas Buenas, PR. June 26.

revitalizing is the missionary zeal of the movement. There is no other event like the *missio Dei* which can testify to the integrality of belief and practice (Jn 12.49).[62] We do not only listen to and believe what God is saying, but we also must act out God's speech to the world in all areas of life. In other words, believers are responsible for acting out God's word to the world. We can also find a similar line of thought in López's work. A church that has believed and experienced the liberating power of the Holy Spirit has the ethical and Christian responsibility to embody in the world what God has done with them. As a matter of fact, just as with Villafañe, López interprets God's love for the world as a missional example for the church. Even more so, López joins the choir as he also stresses how *el culto* (worship service) must be transformative in nature, both in faith and in actions. For López, Pentecostal spirituality has internal and external implications; it may be nurtured within the worshiping community, but it is manifested in all its glory among society.[63]

This integration of faith and practice is possible when the church sees herself as an active participant in society.[64] Unless this happens, the church will only exist in society for herself. Interestingly, contemporary theologians like Karl Barth underscore the importance of the church's integrality of faith and practice. In *The Holy Spirit and the Christian Life*, Barth states the following: 'Faith cannot stand alone: it is always in this and that action self-authenticating, or it is simply not authenticating faith ... That faith has action alongside itself means identically the same thing, namely, that faith is active.'[65] Furthermore, he also elevates the place of sanctification. Through it, we are responsible to act on behalf of our neighbors.[66] To cite Barth,

[T]his means that our sanctification is actual in the fact that we are challenged as responsible beings by a summons that is never suspended but that is to the effect that we are appointed to establish the orders of creation that apply to our existence as such ... in

---

[62] In this verse, there is a movement from that which we received from God to our responsibility to speak and act on that which has been given.

[63] López, *La fiesta del Espíritu*, pp. 43–45.

[64] To have an impact within the greater public sphere, the church needs to see herself as an integrated voice within the other voices that are speaking in society. See Valentin, *Mapping Public Theology*.

[65] Karl Barth, *The Holy Spirit and the Christian Life: The Theological Basis of Ethics* (Louisville, KY: Westminster John Knox Press, 1993), p. 33.

[66] Barth, *The Holy Spirit and the Christian Life*, p. 34.

the church and in the state, in the spiritual and secular order of life implied in the kingdom of grace.[67]

For Barth, there is an intrinsic connection between faith and practice. This integral character comes through the agency of the Holy Spirit in the individual and the community. It is through the Holy Spirit in us that we become conscious of our actions toward God and the world.

Prayer and Intercession as Missiological in Nature

Along with singing *coritos* (songs), prayer and intercession take most of the liturgical space within the Latin American *culto* (worship service). In the words of Catholic theologian Allan Figueroa Deck, 'Much of what is most distinctive in the religious heritage of Hispanic Americans is expressed in the vast gamut of symbols, rituals, and stories around which their life of prayer and worship revolves'.[68] Similarly, Pentecostal theologian Samuel Solivan states that prayer of all sorts is at the heart of Pentecostal Hispanic worship.[69] In tune with both, RAV was no stranger to this reality.

What is most telling from members about RAV's prayer and intercession is their missiological nature. For RAV, prayer and intercession are not solely personal events, but communal. They are not only for the church but also for those outside of the church. 'When we pray', states pastor Willy, 'we stand in the gap for others, and we are living in a moment where our nation needs us to stand in the gap [to pray and intercede] for them'.[70] In other words, for RAV, prayer and intercession must affect that which is happening outside of the church. Through prayer and intercession, the Holy Spirit helps the church identify the public spheres that need transformation. Thus, it was not out of the ordinary that during my visit, amid an economic and political depression, I heard an array of personal, communal, and concerted prayers and intercessions for the sake of the Puerto Rican

---

[67] Barth, *The Holy Spirit and the Christian Life*, p. 34.

[68] Allan Figueroa Deck, S.J., 'Hispanic Catholic Prayer and Worship', in Justo L. González (ed.), *¡Alabadle!: Hispanic Christian Worship* (Nashville: Abingdon Press, 1996), pp. 29–30.

[69] Deck, S.J., 'Hispanic Catholic Prayer and Worship', pp. 43–55 and Estrada-Carrasquillo, 'Taking the Risk: The Openness and Attentiveness of Latin American Pentecostal Worship', pp. 235–46.

[70] Pastor Willy. 2016. Focus group interview by author. Aguas Buenas, PR. June 21.

national crisis. I repeatedly heard expressions like, 'Though the world is in crisis and our civil leaders do not know what to do, God is still on his throne, and to Him we pray'.[71]

Of the three Pentecostal theologians studied, Luvis is the only one who highlighted the importance of prayer and intercession in this manner. For her, the people's prayers have a dual intention. First, the church has an undeniable responsibility to pray for that which is expected to happen in the public sphere. Thus, prayer is not only for the sake of the local church community but also for the sake of the place where the church is located. Second, states Luvis, prayer and intercession move the church to stand as a beacon of hope for society, in a spiritual and material sense. Hence, prayer and intercession, rather than static and disengaged spiritual disciplines, are dynamic and offered on behalf of the entire created order.

During the World Consultation on Frontier Missions (Edinburgh 1980), the theme of prayer was discussed as a central tenet for missions. One of the speakers, Patrick Johnstone, gave a presentation entitled 'Mission Imperative: Intercession'.[72] In this presentation Johnstone affirmed that regardless of how well missionaries and mission organizations have developed a missionary plan, prayer and intercession must take precedence. He expands, 'Unless we see that the only way we can move ahead is on our knees, we are not going to see those breakthroughs'.[73] Moreover, just as stated above by RAV members, Johnstone underscores the correlation between prayer and the work of the Holy Spirit. It is prayer, according to Johnstone, that has propelled the major movements of the Holy Spirit in the world, which can be attested in Scripture and in history. And the Pentecostal movement is no stranger to this, as one of the common elements among global Pentecostal revivals is the role of prayer and intercession. Furthermore, Johnstone, similarly to Luvis, highlights the dynamic nature of prayer. He explains that prayer has to be a prevailing task; we ought to pray

> that kind of praying that goes through until we get an answer. Too often we say prayers and don't expect an answer ... But prevailing

---

[71] 2016. Observation notes by author. Aguas Buenas, PR. May 27.

[72] See Patrick Johnstone, 'Mission Imperative: Intercession' in Allan Starling, *Seeds of Promise: World Consultation on Frontier Missions, Edinburgh '80* (Chicago: William Carey Library, 1981), pp. 193–202.

[73] Starling, *Seeds of Promise*, pp. 195.

prayer is getting what God wants us to pray about and pressing through until we have the certainty in our hearts of the answer even before we necessarily see it.[74]

Prayer and intercession, being missiological in nature, attune the heart of the church to the needs of the community. They help us see and listen to the voice of those in need. Furthermore, the act of praying for them consequently raises the visibility of the church in the world. In the words of Avery Dulles, a praying and interceding church is 'a sign of the continuing vitality of the grace of Christ and of hope for the redemption that he promises'.[75]

The Prophethood of All

Both the prophet and the prophetess along with the office of the prophethood play an essential role throughout the biblical narrative. They had an undeniable responsibility to speak and act on behalf of God for the sake of their community and the surrounding nations. Moreover, and important to this study, such God-led speech and action have in their core a missional mandate, a call of God for the sake of Israel and the other nations, whether to affirm their relationship with God or to return to his presence. Also, key to the work of the prophets, according to Walter Brueggemann, is that regardless of bearing a transcendent divine message, they shared the message in a concrete context.[76]

Pentecostal theologian Roger Stronstad has challenged the Pentecostal community to look within biblical and early Pentecostal history and recover the prophethood of all believers.[77] For Stronstad, there has been much weight placed on the priestly role of the church then and now.[78] Yet, states Stronstad, in Luke's charismatic theology, there is a sense of revitalizing the role of prophethood, though this has been overshadowed by Paul's and the Protestant paradigm of the

---

[74] Starling, *Seeds of Promise*, pp. 197.

[75] Avery Dulles, *Models of the Church* (New York, NY: Image Books, expanded edn, 2002), p. 84.

[76] Brueggemann, *The Prophetic Imagination*.

[77] For example, see Roger Stronstad, *The Charismatic Theology of St. Luke: Trajectories From the Old Testament to Luke-Acts* (Grand Rapids, MI: Baker Academic, 2nd edn, 2012); Roger Stronstad, *The Prophethood of All Believers: A Study in Luke's Charismatic Theology* (JPTSup 16; Sheffield: Sheffield Academic Press, 1999); Roger Stronstad, 'Affirming Diversity: God's People as a Community of Prophets', *Pneuma* 17.2 (September 1995), pp. 145–57.

[78] Stronstad, 'Affirming Diversity', p. 145.

'priesthood of all believers'.[79] This Lukan paradigm underscores that, in short, those who were baptized in the Spirit 'truly functioned as a nation of prophets – the prophethood of all believers by works which were empowered by the Spirit and by words which were empowered by the Spirit'.[80] The importance of the prophethood of all for today lies in that the Spirit-led church is challenged to move *toward* the public sphere. Stronstad argues, 'As a prophetic community, God's people are to be active in service'.[81] In other words, this implies the recuperation of a world-centered ministry.[82]

Accordingly, RAV members see themselves as a community of prophets. Whatever gifts they have been given are for the service of the greater community. This theme of prophethood is intrinsically connected to the theme of prayer and intercession as missiological in nature. For them, it is not only about standing in the gap through prayers (as priest), it 'is also about giving; having compassion':[83] to speak and act for the sake of the Other (as prophets). Furthermore, RAV community describes itself as a church with open doors. Such a descriptor heightens, on the one hand, the hospitable character towards those that visit and on the other hand, their role as prophets. They understand, as Stronstad states, that the Holy Spirit has baptized them, and through that baptism they are thrust into the city.[84] Thus, as part of their Spirit-filled life, they have developed a Spirit-lead public discourse and embodiment. Additionally, RAV is not oblivious to the double nature of this prophetic responsibility. As RAV's missionary to Argentina states, the church's prophetic work brings with it a responsibility to sustain what we say and enact with

---

[79] Stronstad, 'Affirming Diversity', p. 145.

[80] Stronstad, 'Affirming Diversity', p. 153.

[81] Stronstad, *The Prophethood of All Believers*, p. 123.

[82] Regarding this point, Stronstad, 'Affirming Diversity', p. 156, expands,

As a further result of not understanding that their experience is prophetic – which is necessarily others-directed – the Pentecostal's experience tends to be both individualistic, self-centered, and, even, narcissistic. In other words, the experience is sought as a private blessing, rather than as an empowering for ministry. Far too many Pentecostals have been led to receive the blessing of the Holy Spirit in the prayer room and have never been taught to take the empowering of that gift into the streets and marketplaces of society.

[83] Carmen, 2016. Focus group interview by author. Aguas Buenas, PR. May 27.

[84] For all, the same transforming agent, the Holy Spirit, becomes the source of their missional thrust. Yet these are manifested differently: for Carmen, in compassion; for Antonio, in gratitude; for Ricardo, in the modeling of the pastors; and for Pedro, in the natural relationship between his lived faith and lived spaces.

our testimony as the community of the Spirit. Our prophetic speech and actions will always circle back to our testimony in the Spirit.

This idea of prophethood and service is also present in the thought of the theologians consulted. Similar to Stronstad, Villafañe understands that Pentecostals have cast a shadow over the prophetic character of their spirituality, to such an extent that the preaching of the gospel has become an *intra nos* event, with little to no impact on society. Consequently, Villafañe calls for the need to recover *diakonia* (service) within Pentecostalism. In other words, the Pentecostal community is a *sierva* (servant) of the community where she is established. For Villafañe, this servant nature of the Pentecostal community heightens the idea of *solidaridad* (solidarity) for both the individual and the community.[85]

For López, there is no way that a local church that seeks to become public can achieve such a goal unless the members understand themselves as prophets and prophetesses. López observes three kinds of church responses to the public space: rejection, opportunism, and service. Those who reject the public space describe themselves as apolitical, not interested in taking any part, yet the mere rejection of the public sphere is a political stance. Then there are those who seek to be public for the sake of taking advantage of the public realm. Rather than the result of being completely committed to the public space, their involvement is based on their personal agenda and needs.[86] Finally, other churches have understood their role as servants. This service is not uncritical, however. It is qualified by kingdom ethics; not the ruling of one over the others but the disposition of putting the needs of the Other first.

The importance of the prophetic character of the Christian community in the world is also affirmed by voices outside of the Pentecostal tradition. For example, Paul Tillich affirms the prophetic

---

[85] Solidarity. This call by Villafañe to be a prophetic church is not the predicament of our responsibility as priests. See chapter 3.

[86] See, for example, Raimundo Barreto Jr., 'The Church and Society Movement and the Roots of Public Theology in Brazilian Protestantism', *IJPT* 6.1 (January 2012), pp. 70–98. Moreover, commenting on nonparticipation, Karl Barth says, 'Christian activity in the political realm should be guided by the limits of its own mission. However, the church should not be one that 'never wakes from the sleep of an otherwise non-political existence' and only participates when 'questions of religious and ethical nature in the narrower sense are under discussion'. Karl Barth, *Community, State, and Church; Three Essays* (New York: Doubleday, 1960), p. 185.

character of the church in society: 'The church's prophetic word must be heard against ... forms of inhumanity and injustice, but first of all the church must transform the given social structure within itself'.[87] In other words, the church's authority to speak into such issues comes when she speaks first to herself (as stated above). Such cultural engagement springs forth from the love that is manifested in the church through the presence of the spiritual community. Tillich underscores, 'A claim for political, social, and economic equality cannot be derived directly from the character of a church as a community. But it does follow from the church's character as a community of love.'[88] Thus the prophetic character of the church is both intra and interrelated.

Another theologian who understands the centrality of this theme is Jürgen Moltmann. He presents two sides of the prophetic ministry. In the first, Moltmann states that the church needs to be aware of the magical elements within 'political and civil religions', and such awareness needs to develop a prophetic voice capable of criticizing the 'state ideologies, which are supposed to create unity at the cost of liberty'.[89] This view of the prophetic character is the judgment of the wrongdoing of society. The second view of prophetic responsibility does not speak critically of society, but it speaks into society in favor of the needs of those who have been oppressed and marginalized. Moltmann adds, such an approach 'has always tried to act as spokesman for the victims of violence, and to become the public voice of the voiceless'.[90]

Furthermore, Catholic theologian Leonardo Boff makes a powerful statement regarding the prophetic and servant nature of the local church. In *Ecclesiogenesis* he states the following about *base Christian communities*. First, these communities, as any other church, are called in the power of the Holy Spirit. In these communities, there is a sense of equity, as stated by Luvis, and that 'a basic equality of all persons is assumed'.[91] Therefore, the work of the Holy Spirit in the church

---

[87] Paul Tillich, *Systematic Theology, Vol. 3: Life and the Spirit: History and the Kingdom of God* (University of Chicago Press, 1976), Kindle Location 3378.

[88] Paul Tillich, *Systematic Theology, Vol. 3*, Kindle loc. 3374.

[89] Jürgen Moltmann, *God for a Secular Society: The Public Relevance of Theology* (Minneapolis: Fortress Press, 1999), p. 44.

[90] Moltmann, *God for a Secular Society*, p. 58.

[91] Leonardo Boff, *Ecclesiogenesis: The Base Communities Reinvent the Church* (Maryknoll, NY: Orbis Books, 1986), p. 27.

and the communities' orientation to the equality (prophethood) of all has serious and important implications for the work of the local church in the community. In agreement with Stronstad, Boff states first that 'all are sent'.[92] He follows by saying that, as such, 'all must bare prophetic witness', just as the Holy Spirit has done for all.[93] In short, the church is a community of *diakonia*, a community of service, a prophethood of all.

Conclusion

Let us conclude by summarizing the important findings that surfaced in the previous discussion. First, Pentecostals have a unique theological content and a unique theological method. This method, rather than being uniform, is varied. Yet, regardless of its variations, the examples presented above have a common thread: they affirm the role of experience, are true to the movement's ethos and epistemology, are integrative in nature and character, uphold the roles of praxis and context, and are geared to the existential questions of the community. These elements, taken as a whole, serve as a foundation for a Pentecostal contextual theology model.

Second, with this methodological sketch in mind, Pentecostal lived ecclesiology, in conversation with the theologies of Luvis, Villafañe, and López, as well as those from the broader Christian communion, and the themes that surfaced from the ethnography, illustrates that, rather than starting from theory, this ecclesiology takes as its starting point the experiences of *el culto pentecostal* (i.e. local ecclesiology). It was established that Pentecostal churches that seek to be attuned to the public sphere are those that embody the following practices: 1) a non-individualistic understanding of conversion; and 2) a theological understanding that conversion is not only a God act that saves the church *from* the world but also thrusts believers *toward* the world.

---

[92] Boff, *Ecclesiogenesis*, p. 27. Regarding this idea of *all*, Stronstad explains that Moses' statement – of all being full of the Spirit, just as the seventy (Num. 11.29) – is fulfilled in the Lukan literature as there is a progression from Elizabeth, Mary, John, and Jesus; to the one hundred and twenty; and to the nations. See Stronstad, 'Affirming Diversity'.

[93] Boff, *Ecclesiogenesis*, p. 27.

In addition, Pentecostal churches that seek to become public need to recover the integrated nature and character of Pentecostal spirituality. Just as with conversion, a Spirit-filled church has an intrinsic call to move into the public sphere and become agents of liberation and freedom, as experienced personally; just as the agency of the Spirit made a way for Jesus to move into our *barrio* (the world), the church in the power of the Holy Spirit must move into every public sphere.

Furthermore, a Pentecostal lived ecclesiology affirms the role of prayer and intercession for the task at hand, as well as the missiological nature of both. Jesus understood this and modeled it; before sending his disciples out, he prayed for them. He knew that prayer and intercession on behalf of the disciples was key for the world to believe and be transformed (John 17).

Finally, another characteristic was that of the prophethood of all. In this, we can see the fulfilment of the previous three. Affirming the prophethood of all is not meant as a rejection of the priesthood of the church. Yet the baptism of the Holy Spirit gives the church the boldness to speak and act God's word. This is not only a reappropriation of the biblical narrative but also an affirmation of the heart of the early Pentecostal movement.

6

CONCLUSION AND CONTRIBUTIONS

Testimonies from members of *RAV* illustrate the church's Mission. Manual states,

> We are an open-door church. Open? Yes! Because the one who comes through our doors is not rejected. People can arrive as they wish, and we are not scandalized because the one who transforms is the Holy Spirit. The Spirit is the one who restores them. Open? Yes! Because we constantly go out, and participate in community events, such as Relay for Life or Antique Car Festival. This church is part of our community.[1]

María says,

> As a church we do not presume that we are the most holy. We are ordinary people who want to live our faith. We are not afraid to walk with the needy – regardless of their state – and bear witness to them. We are not only seeking to be present; we hope to see transformation.[2]

Antonio asks,

> What about the prison guard who became friends with an inmate? That relationship grew in a very special way in a space beyond the church building. And when this man left jail, he decided that he wanted to come to the church of his friend – the prison guard. A public institution became a sphere of redemption due to the

---

[1] Manuel. 2016. Focus group interview by author. Aguas Buenas, PR. July 10.
[2] María. 2016. Focus group interview by author. Aguas Buenas, PR. July 10.

Christian life modeled by the prison guard, a member of our church.[3]

Behold!

Testimonies like these depict what RAV church is in its essence: it is a church when people are gathered together, and it remains a church when they are scattered throughout the city. In other words, RAV embodies a *culto*-like ecclesiology that integrates its Pentecostal spirituality with the public sphere. A lived ecclesiology informed by a conversation that integrates spirituality and the public sphere does not merely conform with the advocacy and dialogue proposed by public theology. The type of lived ecclesiology that is proposed in this study calls for further responsibility and contextuality; that is, closing the gap between the temple and the city by sending the church community – like streams of water – in the power of the Holy Spirit to live out the kingdom of God in the time and place of present need.

If a Pentecostal lived ecclesiology is like the stream of water that constantly flows from the temple to the city, as in Ezekiel's vision, then this calls for a reinterpretation of the long-standing dichotomy between public and private that undergirds the discussion within public theology. Some voices within the area of public theology have proposed something similar. For example, in *Mapping Public Theology*, Benjamin Valentin argues that the church does not live outside of the city. As part of the city, she cannot see herself as a body beyond the public sphere but lives as part of it.[4] Also, Ronald F. Thiemann makes a similar argument in *Constructing a Public Theology*.[5] He argues that public theology needs to come down from its 'general philosophical or metaphysical argumentation' and become rooted in particular – that is, concrete – events.[6] Nevertheless, though their criticism is well received, their proposals still remain within the confines of a discursive approach and do not move into the embodiment of a lived theology. Furthermore, public theology seems to have a docetic soteriological undertone: separating the material needs of the people from

---

[3] Antonio. 2016. Focus group interview by author. Aguas Buenas, PR. July 10.

[4] See Valentin, *Mapping Public Theology*.

[5] Ronald F. Thiemann, *Constructing a Public Theology: The Church in a Pluralistic Culture* (Louisville, KY: Westminster/John Knox Press, 1991).

[6] Thiemann is speaking in criticism of David Tracy's approach to public theology. Thiemann, *Constructing a Public Theology*, p. 21.

their spiritual needs.[7] However, a lived ecclesiology informed by a Pentecostal spirituality has a broader and more wholistic soteriological approach, grounded in a pneumatological christology that not only confronts but also brings healing to the structural, social/communal, and human spheres.

In short, a Pentecostal lived ecclesiology that embodies the kingdom of God seeks to nurture, propitiate, and foster – in the power of the Holy Spirit – an integral transformation. As in Ezekiel 47, it is not only about how far the waters have extended from the door of the temple but also about how the water that flows 'from the sanctuary' (v. 12) needs to bear the fruit of transformation wherever it goes.

Contributions

Let me suggest how this study contributes to the literature of Pentecostal, contextual, and public theologies in particular and to missiological studies as whole.

First, the study argues for a reinterpretation of the relationship between the church and society. In other words, rather than pitting the sacred and the public against each other, this study promotes an integrative understanding of faith and life. Such a proposal brings a fresh understanding within the area of contextual studies. Pentecostals – in this case, Latin American – favor an integral spirituality that stands against the Western-favored dichotomy between the private and the public. This integral spirituality of Latino/a Pentecostals responds to two important elements: (1) the wholistic social imaginary that permeates in the Majority World[8] and (2) to the ubiquitous Pentecostal understanding of what it means to live a Spirit-filled life. At times, literature on contextual theology has misrepresented or portrayed Pentecostals as a people that has no footing here and now, as looking up to heaven and avoiding any interventions with society. However, in recent years Pentecostal scholarship has responded to such misinterpretations, and in a way, this study seeks to join the choir

---

[7] In principle, Docetism is a doctrine that differentiates between Jesus' divinity and physical body. For those who uphold this doctrine, divinity and humanity could not integrate.

[8] William A. Dyrness, *Learning about Theology from the Third World* (Grand Rapids, MI: Academie Books, Zondervan, 1990).

by proposing a contextual theology and methodology from a Latino/a Pentecostal perspective and a lived ecclesiology.[9]

Second, the study seeks to make a contribution to mission studies by arguing, in agreement with Stanley H. Skreslet, that studies within this area must be hospitable to interdisciplinary conversations.[10] Though the church is not of the world, she is in it. And the beauty of the divine dwells among the fragility of humanity. Hence, the church is not a neat or passive context. It is a messy and dynamic reality. Such reality calls for a multifaceted conversation according to the topic at hand. Thus, studies focusing on the nature and mission of the church call for the collaboration of multiple perspectives. This study brings together contributions from Pentecostal, contextual, and public theologies. To this point, no study has intentionally demonstrated that these loci have much to offer in unison, especially within the landscape of Latino/a Pentecostalism. The interlocution of these three branches of theology developed a trialectical relationship that goes against a mutually exclusive understanding of any of them. Though such a trialectical relationship was seen in light of the construction of a Latino/a Pentecostal lived ecclesiology, I understand that the scholarship may benefit from the interconnectedness that exists among these theological loci as they are applied in other areas of study.

Third, the study contributes to the area of theological studies by giving prominence to the local liturgy and to the voice of the congregants that participate in it. In the introductory comments in *Explorations in Ecclesiology and Ethnography*, Christian Scharen comments that until recently, studies on the church suffered from the divide between scholarship and the worshipers.[11] Following a similar line of thought, in *Local Theology for the Global Church*, Rob Haskell questions if 'we simply translate tried and true theological notions from one culture to another or do we encourage each culture to do its own theologizing based on its own questions and priorities?'[12] In response

---

[9] A. Scott Moreau, 'Evangelical Models of Contextualization' in Cook, *Local Theology for the Global Church*, Kindle, 5842. In his concluding comments, Moreau attests that his work is not concluded. He affirms that new voices and contextual models will develop, specifically from a Pentecostal perspective.

[10] Skreslet, *Comprehending Mission*, pp. 11, 16.

[11] Christian Scharen (ed.), *Explorations in Ecclesiology and Ethnography* (Studies in Ecclesiology and Ethnography; Grand Rapids, MI: Eerdmans, 2012), p. 1.

[12] Cook, *Local Theology for the Global Church*, Kindle, p. 123.

to this challenge and following the work of Mark Cartledge on Pentecostal ecclesiology, this study not only focuses on how the congregants participate, interact with, interpret, and live their faith in their everyday experiences, but it also is concerned with how these local voices reinterpret theological discourses. This *carnal ecclesiology* not only nuances theology proper but, more importantly, opens a space for new theological categories (see Chapter 5) that arise from particular experiences.[13]

Finally, the study offers a Latino/a and Pentecostal contribution to the developing area of public missiology.[14] According to Sebastian Kim, the goal of public missiology is the 'transformation of society' through 'advocacy' or 'words and deeds'.[15] Furthermore, as Gregory Leffel states, such transformation occurs through a 'discernable community'.[16] Following this line of thought, the study demonstrated that this public and missional character can been seen not only in the works of Luvis, Villafañe, and López (Chapter 3) but also in the life and ministry of RAV church (Chapter 4). As a result, I have proposed a Latino/a Pentecostal lived ecclesiology that seeks to explain how lived faith is embodied in lived spaces for the sake of the transformation of the public sphere (Chapter 5). This is possible because Pentecostal theology and spirituality is intrinsically imbued with public and missional undertones. As Allan Anderson affirms, 'Just as Spirit baptism is Pentecostalism's central, most distinctive doctrine, so mission is Pentecostalism's central, most important activity'.[17]

Moving Forward

Before concluding, one final comment regarding future research is advisable. This study argues that Pentecostal ecclesiology – in the Latino/a context – demonstrates an integral spirituality and a public-oriented liturgy that moves seamlessly between the sanctuary and the city. However, considering the plethora of Pentecostal expressions

---

[13] Sharen and Vigen describe their work as a 'carnal theology'. That is, a theology that is embodied. Following their line of thought, I suggest the term 'carnal ecclesiology'. See Christian Scharen and Aana Marie Vigen (eds.), *Ethnography as Christian Theology and Ethics* (New York: Continuum, 2011), p. 30.

[14] See, for example, Gregory Leffel, 'The "public" of a Missiology of Public Life: Actors and Opportunities', *Missiology* 44.2 (April 2016), pp. 167–79.

[15] Sebastian C.H. Kim, 'Mission's Public Engagement: The Conversation of Missiology and Public Theology', *Missiology* 45.1 (2017), pp. pp. 12–13.

[16] Leffel, 'The 'Public' of a Missiology of Public Life', p. 170.

[17] Anderson, *Spreading Fires*, p. 65.

globally, it will be necessary to implement a similar case study methodology in a non-Latino/a or non-Caribbean context and analyze the similarities and differences between these studies. I hope that future students and fellow scholars may join in this venture.

Let us flow into the city!

BIBLIOGRAPHY

Alexander, Kimberly Ervin, *Pentecostal Healing: Models in Theology and Practice* (JPTSup 29; Blandford Forum: Deo Publishing, 2006).

Alfaro, Sammy, *Divino Compañero: Toward a Hispanic Pentecostal Christology* (Eugene, OR: Wipf & Stock, 2010).

Althouse, Peter, 'Towards a Pentecostal Ecclesiology: Participation in the Missional Life of the Triune God', *Journal of Pentecostal Theology* 18.2 (September 2009), pp. 230–45.

Álvarez, Miguel, 'Contextualización de La Hermenéutica Latina', *Hechos* 1.1 (Jan 2019), pp. 3–17.

Anderson, Allan, *Spreading Fires: The Missionary Nature of Early Pentecostalism* (Maryknoll, NY: Orbis Books, 2007).

Archer, Kenneth J., *A Pentecostal Hermeneutic: Spirit, Scripture, and Community* (Cleveland, TN: CPT Press, 2009).

—'A Pentecostal Way of Doing Theology: Method and Manner', *International Journal of Systematic Theology* 9.3 (July 2007), pp. 301–14.

—'Nourishment for Our Journey: The Pentecostal *Via Salutis* and Sacramental Ordiances', *Journal of Pentecostal Theology* 13.1 (October 1, 2004), pp. 79–96.

Archer, Melissa L., *'I Was in the Spirit on the Lord's Day': A Pentecostal Engagement with Worship in the Apocalypse* (Cleveland, TN: CPT Press, 2015).

Barreto Jr., Raimundo, 'The Church and Society Movement and the Roots of Public Theology in Brazilian Protestantism', *International Journal of Public Theology* 6.1 (January 2012), pp. 70–98.

Barth, Karl, *Community, State, and Church; Three Essays* (New York: Doubleday, 1960).

—*The Holy Spirit and the Christian Life: The Theological Basis of Ethics* (Louisville, KY: Westminster John Knox Press, 1993).

Basdeo Hill, A. Rebecca, *Visions of God in Ezekiel: Pentecostal Explorations of the Glory and Holiness of Yahweh* (Cleveland, TN: CPT Press, 2018).

Boff, Leonardo, *Ecclesiogenesis: The Base Communities Reinvent the Church* (Maryknoll, NY: Orbis Books, 1986).

Brueggemann, Walter, *The Prophetic Imagination* (Minneapolis, MN: Fortress Press, 2nd edn, 2001).

Cartledge, Mark J., *Narratives and Numbers: Empirical Studies of Pentecostal and Charismatic Christianity* (Global Pentecostal and Charismatic Studies 24; Leiden: Brill, 2017).

—'Pentecostal Theological Method and Intercultural Theology', *Transformation* 25.2/3 (April 2008), pp. 92–102.

—'Renewal Ecclesiology in Empirical Perspective', *Pneuma* 36.1 (2014), pp. 5–24.

'Censo 2010 Puerto Rico' (Departamento de Comercio de EE.UU., 2012). www.census.gov.

Chiquete, Daniel, *Silencio elocuente: una interpretación de la arquitectura pentecostal* (San José, Costa Rica: Univ. Bíblica Latinoamericana, 2006).

Church of God General Assembly Minutes (Cleveland, TN: Church of God Publishing House, 1913).

Constructive Christian Theology, The Workgroup. *Constructive Theology: A Contemporary Approach to Classic Themes: A Project of The Workgroup on Constructive Christian Theology* (Minneapolis: Augsburg Fortress Publishers, 2005).

Cook, Matthew (ed.), *Local Theology for the Global Church: Principles for an Evangelical Approach to Contextualization* (Pasadena: World Evangelical Alliance Theological Commission, 2010).

Costas, Orlando E., *The Integrity of Mission: The Inner Life and Outreach the Church* (San Francisco: Harper & Row, 1979).

Coulter, Dale M., 'Baptism, Conversion, and Grace: Reflections on the 'underlying Realities' between Pentecostals, Methodists, and Catholics', *Pneuma* 31.2 (2009), pp. 189–212.

Cox, Harvey, 'A Review of 'Pentecostal Spirituality: A Passion for the Kingdom', by Steven J Land', *Journal of Pentecostal Theology* 2.5 (October 1994), pp. 3–12.

Cross, Terry L., 'A Proposal to Break the Ice: What Can Pentecostal Theology Offer Evangelical Theology?', *Journal of Pentecostal Theology* 10.2 (April 2002), pp. 44–73.

—'The Rich Feast of Theology: Can Pentecostals Bring the Main Course or Only the Relish?', *Journal of Pentecostal Theology* 16 (April 2000), pp. 27–47.

Dayton, Donald W., *Theological Roots of Pentecostalism* (Peabody, MA: Hendrickson, 1987).

Dulles, Avery, *Models of the Church* (New York, NY: Image Books, Expanded edn, 2002).

Dyrness, William A., *Learning about Theology from the Third World* (Grand Rapids, MI: Academie Books, Zondervan, 1990).

Dyrness, William A., Veli-Matti Kärkkäinen, Juan F. Martinez, and Simon Chan (eds.), *Global Dictionary of Theology: A Resource for the Worldwide Church* (Downers Grove, IL: IVP Academic, 2008).

Engen, Charles Edward van, Darrell L. Whiteman, and John Dudley Woodberry (eds.), *Paradigm Shifts in Christian Witness: Insights from Anthropology,*

Communication, and Spiritual Power: Essays in Honor of Charles H. Kraft (Maryknoll, NY: Orbis Books, 2008).

Espinosa, Gastón, *Latino Pentecostals in America: Faith and Politics in Action* (Cambridge, MA: Harvard University Press, 2014).

Estrada Adorno, Wilfredo, *El Fuego Está Encendido: Infancia Del Pentecostalismo Puertorriqueño y Su Impacto En La Sociedad* (Cleveland, TN: CEL Publicaciones, 2016).

Estrada, Rodolfo Galvan, *A Pneumatology of Race in the Gospel of John: An Ethnocritical Study* (Eugene, OR: Pickwick, 2019).

Estrada-Carrasquillo, Wilmer, *Hacia una eclesiología hispana-latina: Una respuesta al reto de la mcdonalización* (Cleveland, TN: CEL Publicaciones, 2019).

Figueroa Aponte, Miriam E., *Hacia una teología pentecostalista: Mujeres impulsadas por el Espíritu Santo* (CEL Publicaciones, 2016).

Freire, Paulo, *Pedagogy of the Oppressed* (New York: Continuum, 30th Anniv. edn, 2000).

Gause, R. Hollis, *Living in the Spirit: The Way of Salvation* (Cleveland, TN: CPT Press, rev. and expanded edn, 2009).

González, Justo L., *Alabadle!: Hispanic Christian Worship* (Nashville: Abingdon Press, 1996).

—*Mañana: Christian Theology from a Hispanic Perspective* (Nashville: Abingdon Press, 1990).

González, Justo L., and Ondina E. González, *Christianity in Latin America: A History* (New York: Cambridge University Press, 2007).

Green, Chris E.W., *Sanctifying Interpretation: Vocation, Holiness, and Scripture* (Cleveland, TN: CPT Press, 2015).

—*Toward a Pentecostal Theology of the Lord's Supper: Foretasting the Kingdom* (Cleveland, TN: CPT Press, 2012).

Green, Joel B., and Max Turner (eds.), *Between Two Horizons: Spanning New Testament Studies and Systematic Theology* (Grand Rapids, MI: Eerdmans, 1999).

Gutiérrez, Gustavo, *We Drink from Our Own Wells: The Spiritual Journey of a People* (Maryknoll, NY: Orbis Books, 20th Anniv. edn, 2003).

Harris, R. Laird, Gleason L. Archer Jr, and Bruce K. Waltke, *Theological Wordbook of the Old Testament* (Chicago, IL: Moody Publishers, rev. edn, 2003).

Hiebert, Paul G., 'The Category "Christian" in the Mission Task', *International Review of Mission* 72.287 (July 1, 1983), pp. 421–27.

Hollenweger, Walter J., *Pentecostalism: Origins and Developments Worldwide* (Peabody, MA: Hendrickson, 2005).

Hunsberger, George R., *Bearing the Witness of the Spirit: Lesslie Newbigin's Theology of Cultural Plurality* (The Gospel and Our Culture Series; Grand Rapids, MI: Eerdmans, 1998).

Hunter, Harold D., and Neil Ormerod, *The Many Faces of Global Pentecostalism* (Cleveland, TN: CPT Press, 2013).

Jenkins, Philip, *The Next Christendom: The Coming of Global Christianity* (New York: Oxford University Press, 3rd edn, 2011).

Johns, Cheryl Bridges, 'Grieving, Brooding, and Transforming', *Journal of Pentecostal Theology* 23.2 (October 2014), pp. 141–53.

—*Pentecostal Formation: A Pedagogy among the Oppressed* (JPTSup 2; Sheffield: Sheffield Academic Press, 1993).

Johns, Jackie David, and Cheryl Bridges Johns, 'Yielding to the Spirit: A Pentecostal Approach to Group Bible Study', *Journal of Pentecostal Theology* 1.1 (1992), pp. 109–34.

Johnson, David R., *Pneumatic Discernment in the Apocalypse: An Intertextual and Pentecostal Exploration* (Cleveland, TN: CPT Press, 2018).

Kalu, Ogbu U. (ed.), *African Christianity: An African Story* (Trenton, NJ: Africa World Press, 2007).

Kärkkäinen, Veli-Matti, *Toward a Pneumatological Theology: Pentecostal and Ecumenical Perspectives on Ecclesiology, Soteriology, and Theology of Mission* (Lanham, MD: University Press of America, 2002).

Kim, Sebastian C.H., 'Mission's Public Engagement: The Conversation of Missiology and Public Theology', *Missiology* 45.1 (2017), pp. 7–24.

Land, Steven J., 'A Passion for the Kingdom: Revisioning Pentecostal Spirituality', *Journal of Pentecostal Theology* 1.1 (1992), pp. 19–46.

—*Pentecostal Spirituality: A Passion for the Kingdom* (Cleveland, TN: CPT Press, 2010).

Leffel, Gregory, 'The "public" of a Missiology of Public Life: Actors and Opportunities', *Missiology* 44.2 (April 2016), pp. 167–79.

López Rodríguez, Darío, *La fiesta del espíritu: espiritualidad y celebración pentecostal* (Lima: Ediciones Puma, 2006).

—*La propuesta política del Reino de Dios: estudios bíblicos sobre iglesia, sociedad y estado* (Lima, Peru: Ediciones Puma, 2009).

—*Pentecostalismo y misión integral: teología del espíritu, teología de la vida* (Lima, Peru: Ediciones Puma, 2008).

—*Pentecostalismo Y Transformación Social* (Buenos Aires: Ediciones Kairos, 2003).

—*The Liberating Mission of Jesus: The Message of the Gospel of Luke* (Pentecostals, Peacemaking, and Social Justice Series; Eugene, OR: Wipf & Stock, 2012).

López Rodríguez, Darío, and Víctor Arroyo, *Tejiendo un nuevo rostro público* (Lima, Peru: Ediciones Puma, rev. edn, 2014).

López Rodríguez, Darío, and Richard E. Waldrop, 'The God of Life and the Spirit of Life: The Social and Political Dimension of Life in the Spirit', *Studies in World Christianity* 17 (January 1, 2011), pp. 1–11.

Luvis Núñez, Agustina, *Creada a Su Imagen: Ministerio Series AETH: Una Pastoral Integral Para La Mujer* (Nashville: Abingdon Press, 2012).

—'Sewing a New Cloth: A Proposal for a Pentecostal Ecclesiology Fashioned as a Community Gifted by the Spirit with the Marks of the Church from a Latina Perspective' (DMin diss., Lutheran School of Theology, 2009).

Macchia, Frank D., *Bautizado en el espiritu: una teología, pentecostal global* (Miami, FL: Vida, 2008).

—'Towards Individual and Communal Renewal: Reflections on Luke's Theology of Conversion', *Ex Auditu* 25 (2009), pp. 92–105.

Martell-Otero, Loida I., Zaida Maldonado Pérez, Elizabeth Conde-Frazier, and Serene Jones, *Latina Evangélicas: A Theological Survey from the Margins* (Eugene, OR: Cascade Books, 2013).

Martin, Lee Roy (ed.), *Pentecostal Hermeneutics: A Reader* (Leiden: Brill, 2013).

—*Toward a Pentecostal Theology of Worship* (Cleveland, TN: CPT Press, 2015).

McKenzie, Steven L. (ed.), *The Oxford Encyclopedia of Biblical Interpretation* (Oxford: Oxford University Press, 2013).

McKim, Donald K., *Westminster Dictionary of Theological Terms* (Louisville, KY: Westminster John Knox Press, 1996).

Medina, Néstor, and Sammy Alfaro (eds.), *Pentecostals and Charismatics in Latin America and Latino Communities* (Christianity and Renewal-Interdisciplinary Studies; New York: Palgrave Macmillan, 2015).

Moffett, Samuel Hugh, *A History of Christianity in Asia: Beginnings to 1500* (Maryknoll, NY: Orbis Books, 2nd sub. edn, 1998).

Moltmann, Jürgen, *God for a Secular Society: The Public Relevance of Theology* (Minneapolis: Fortress Press, 1999).

Neill, Stephen, *A History of Christian Missions* (ed. Owen Chadwick; London; New York: Penguin Books, 1990).

Newbigin, Lesslie, *The Gospel in a Pluralist Society* (Grand Rapids, MI: Eerdmans, 1989).

Noll, Mark A., *The Scandal of the Evangelical Mind* (Grand Rapids, MI: Eerdmans, 1995).

Oliverio, Jr., L. William, 'An Interpretive Review Essay on Amos Yong's Spirit-Word-Community: Theological Hermeneutics in Trinitarian Perspective', *Journal of Pentecostal Theology* 18.2 (2009), pp. 301–11.

Ott, Craig, and Harold A Netland, *Globalizing Theology: Belief and Practice in an Era of World Christianity* (Grand Rapids, MI: Baker Academic, 2006).

Padilla, C. René, *Mision integral: ensayos sobre el Reino y la iglesia* (Grand Rapids, MI: Eerdmans, 1986).

Pagán, Samuel, *Ezequiel y Daniel* (Minneapolis, MN: Augsburg Fortress, 2010).

Turney, H.M., 'The Baptism of the Holy Spirit', *Pentecostal Evangel* 146 (1916), p. 5.

Richie, Tony, *Toward a Pentecostal Theology of Religions: Encountering Cornelius Today* (Cleveland, TN: CPT Press, 2013).

Scharen, Christian (ed.), *Explorations in Ecclesiology and Ethnography* (Studies in Ecclesiology and Ethnography; Grand Rapids, MI: Eerdmans, 2012).

Scharen, Christian, and Aana Marie Vigen (eds.) *Ethnography as Christian Theology and Ethics* (London: Continuum, 2011).

Schreiter, Robert J., *Constructing Local Theologies* (Maryknoll, NY: Orbis Books, 1985).

Sedmak, Clemens, *Doing Local Theology: A Guide for Artisans of a New Humanity* (Faith and Cultures Series; Maryknoll, NY: Orbis Books, 2002).

Segura, Harold, 'La Misión Integral: Treinta y Cinco Años Después', *Espacio de Diálogo* 2 (April 2005).

S[exton], E.A., 'Editorial: River of Water of Life', *The Bridegroom's Messenger* 3.48 (Oct 15, 1909), p. 1.

Sisson, Miss E., 'Blessings from Under the Threshold: The Vision of the Holy Waters', *The Latter Rain Evangel* 4.9 (June 1912), p. 12.

Skreslet, Stanley H., *Comprehending Mission: The Questions, Methods, Themes, Problems, and Prospects of Missiology* (American Society of Missiology Series 49; Maryknoll, NY: Orbis Books, 2012).

Smith, James K.A., 'Scandalizing Theology: A Pentecostal Response to Noll's Scandal', *Pneuma* 19.2 (September 1997), pp. 225–38.

—*Thinking in Tongues: Pentecostal Contributions to Christian Philosophy* (Pentecostal Manifestos; Grand Rapids, MI: Eerdmans, 2010).

Solivan, Samuel, *The Spirit, Pathos and Liberation: Toward a Hispanic Pentecostal Theology* (JPTSup 14; Sheffield: Sheffield Academic Press, 1998).

Spickard, Paul R., and Kevin M. Cragg, *A Gobal History of Christians: How Everyday Believers Experienced Their World* (Grand Rapids, MI: Baker Books, 2001).

Starling, Allan, *Seeds of Promise: World Consultation on Frontier Missions, Edinburgh '80* (Chicago: William Carey Library, 1981).

Stephenson, Christopher A., *Types of Pentecostal Theology: Method, System, Spirit* (Academy Series; New York: Oxford University Press, 2013).

Streib, Heinz, Astrid Dinter, and Kerstin Söderblom (eds.), *Lived Religion: Conceptual, Empirical and Practical-Theological Approaches: Essays in Honor of Hans-Günter Heimbrock* (Leiden: Brill, 2008).

Stronstad, Roger, 'Affirming Diversity: God's People as a Community of Prophets', *Pneuma* 17.2 (September 1995), pp. 145–57.

—*The Charismatic Theology of St. Luke: Trajectories From the Old Testament to Luke-Acts* (Grand Rapids, MI: Baker Academic, 2nd edn, 2012).

—*The Prophethood of All Believers: A Study in Luke's Charismatic Theology* (JPTSup 16; Sheffield: Sheffield Academic Press, 1999).

Synan, Vinson, *The Century of Holy Spirit: 100 Years of Pentecostal and Charismatic Renewal, 1901-2001* (Nashville: Thomas Nelson, 2012).

—*The Holiness-Pentecostal Tradition: Charismatic Movements in the Twentieth Century* (Grand Rapids, MI: Eerdmans, 2nd edn, 1997).

Taylor, Charles, *Modern Social Imaginaries* (Durham: Duke University Press Books, 2003).

Tennent, Timothy C., *Theology in the Context of World Christianity: How the Global Church Is Influencing the Way We Think about and Discuss Theology* (Grand Rapids, MI: Zondervan, 2007).

Thiemann, Ronald F., *Constructing a Public Theology: The Church in a Pluralistic Culture* (Louisville, KY: Westminster/John Knox Press, 1991).

Thomas, John Christopher, 'Pentecostal Theology in the Twenty-First Century', *Pneuma* 20.1 (1998), pp. 3–19.

—*Toward a Pentecostal Ecclesiology: The Church and the Fivefold Gospel* (Cleveland, TN: CPT Press, 2010).

Thoreau, Henry D., 'Civil Disobedience', 1849. http://thoreau.eserver.org/civil1.html.

Tillich, Paul, *Systematic Theology, Vol. 3: Life and the Spirit: History and the Kingdom of God* (Chicago: University of Chicago Press, 1976).

Valentin, Benjamin, *Mapping Public Theology: Beyond Culture, Identity, and Difference* (Harrisburg, PA: Trinity Press Int'l, 2002).

Villafañe, Eldin, *El Espíritu Liberador: Hacia Una Ética Social Pentecostal Hispanoamericana* (Buenos Aires: Nueva Creación, 1996).

—*Seek the Peace of the City: Reflections on Urban Ministry* (Grand Rapids, MI: Eerdmans, 1995).

—'The Politics of the Spirit: Reflections on a Theology of Social Transformation for the Twenty-First Century', *Pneuma* 18.2 (September 1, 1996), pp. 161–70.

Vondey, Wolfgang, 'The Making of a Black Liturgy: Pentecostal Worship and Spirituality from African Slave Narratives to American Cityscapes', *Black Theology* 10.2 (August 2012), pp. 147–68.

—'Types of Pentecostal Theology: Method, System, Spirit', *Pneuma* 37.1 (2015), pp. 160–62.

Walls, Andrew F., *The Cross-Cultural Process in Christian History: Studies in the Transmission and Appropriation of Faith* (Maryknoll, NY: Orbis Books, 2002).

—*The Missionary Movement in Christian History: Studies in the Transmission of Faith* (Maryknoll, NY: Orbis Books, 1996).

Ward, Peter, *Perspectives on Ecclesiology and Ethnography* (Studies in Ecclesiology and Ethnography; Eerdmans, 2012).

Williams, Rowan, *The Edge of Words: God and the Habits of Language* (London: Bloomsbury, 2014).

Wright, Christopher J.H., *The Mission of God: Unlocking the Bible's Grand Narrative* (Downers Grove, IL: IVP Academic, 2006).

Yong, Amos, *In the Days of Caesar: Pentecostalism and Political Theology* (The Cadbury Lectures 2009; Grand Rapids, MI: Eerdmans, 2010).

—*Spirit, Word, Community: Theological Hermeneutics in Trinitarian Perspective* (Eugene, OR: Wipf & Stock, 2006).

—'The Hermeneutical Trialectic: Notes Toward a Consensual Hermeneutic and Theological Method', *Heythrop Journal* 45.1 (January 2004), pp. 22–39.

Zizioulas, John D., *Being as Communion: Studies in Personhood and the Church* (Crestwood, NY: St Vladimir's Seminary Press, 1997).

INDEX OF BIBLICAL REFERENCES

Index of Authors